THE RED WAVE

THE NEW POLITICS REVIEW OF THE 2025 AUSTRALIAN FEDERAL ELECTION

EDDY JOKOVICH + DAVID LEWIS

The Red Wave: The New Politics review of the 2025 Australian federal election
ISBN (paperback): 978-1-7-635701-4-6
ISBN (Amazon):   979-8-2-843818-1-6

©2025 Eddy Jokovich & David Lewis

All rights reserved. No part of this book may be reproduced in any form or by any electronic or mechanical means, including information storage and retrieval systems, without written permission from the authors, except for the use of brief quotations in book reviews and promotional material.

May 2025.
Published by New Politics, an imprint of ARMEDIA Pty. Ltd.

New Politics
PO Box 1265, Darlinghurst NSW 1300
www.newpolitics.com.au
Email: info@newpolitics.com.au

Production: ARMEDIA

Published and produced on the lands of the Wangal and Gadigal people.

EDITORIAL NOTE ON THE USE OF AI TECHNOLOGY
We employ artificial intelligence tools in the editing process of our articles. These tools assisted with transcriptions of audio recordings, grammar correction, refinement and formatting.

A catalogue record for this work is available from the National Library of Australia

CONTENTS

PROLOGUE	The year of the election	6
CHAPTER 1	The calm before the storm	10
CHAPTER 2	On track for a dirty and divisive campaign	19
CHAPTER 3	Unhappy Australia Day and blocking Reconciliation	29
CHAPTER 4	The chaos and unravelling of an American democracy	36
CHAPTER 5	The descent into Trumpism and the failure to fight back	45
CHAPTER 6	Albanese's gamble on U.S. tariffs	52
CHAPTER 7	Australia keeps failing to Close the Gap	59
CHAPTER 8	Manufacturing outrage with Zionist provocateurs	66
CHAPTER 9	Australia's poll frenzy and unbelievable pro-Dutton spin	75
CHAPTER 10	The cracks in the empire: America's allies drift away	84
CHAPTER 11	A better economy but did Labor sell the good news?	93
CHAPTER 12	Manufacturing fear: Fake terror as a political weapon	102
CHAPTER 13	Dutton's disaster: How a cyclone exposed his leadership	110
CHAPTER 14	The Budget myth: How outrage skewed the debate	119
CHAPTER 15	The federal election campaign commences	128

CHAPTER 16	Labor's momentum and a shaky start for the Coalition	133
CHAPTER 17	Dutton's disastrous start to the campaign	140
CHAPTER 18	The election fear and paranoia circus act	147
CHAPTER 19	How Dutton's campaign started to fall apart	152
CHAPTER 20	The silence of the ballot box: Ignoring Gaza	163
CHAPTER 21	A masterclass in political failure	170
CHAPTER 22	The fiction of fixing Australia's housing crisis	181
CHAPTER 23	A strange, disjointed week in the campaign end game	191
CHAPTER 24	How cost of living fear was shaped for political gain	202
CHAPTER 25	Culture wars and the politics of desperation	209
CHAPTER 26	Remembering the ghosts of 2019	214
CHAPTER 27	Election night: A historic victory and a devastating loss	221
CHAPTER 28	The collapse of a party: What's next for the Liberals?	229
CHAPTER 29	The power of the mandate	237
EPILOGUE		244

ABOUT THE AUTHORS

EDDY JOKOVICH is editor of *New Politics*, and co-presenter of the New Politics Australia podcast. He has worked as a journalist, publisher, author, political analyst, campaigner, war correspondent, and lecturer in media studies at the University of Technology, Sydney and the University of Sydney; has a wide range of experience working in editorial and media production work and is Director of ARMEDIA, an independent publishing and communications company specialising in public interest media.

DAVID LEWIS is co-presenter of the New Politics Australia podcast, historian, musicologist, musician and political scientist based in Sydney. His lecturing and research interests include roots music, popular music, Australian, U.K. and U.S. politics and crime fiction. He has published in *Music Forum Australia*, *Eureka Street*, *Quadrant*, *Crikey* and has edited several books.

NEW POLITICS AUSTRALIA is a weekly podcast, providing analysis and opinions on Australia politics. It can be found at Apple Podcasts, Spotify and Amazon Audible.

PROLOGUE: THE YEAR OF THE ELECTION

It was an endless summer of heat, discomfort and discontent in many parts of the country. As Australia emerged from the long tail of 2024 and stepped into the new year with some sense of optimism, the feeling of unease was clear. Like all previous elections, the 2025 federal election wasn't going to be just another contest for power—it was a test of political endurance, ideology and national identity.

For the Labor government, elected in 2022 with great hope and anticipation, this parliamentary term had been steady but unremarkable. As promised, Prime Minister Anthony Albanese had governed with caution and competence, avoiding scandals but failing to inspire the public. His government had held the country together in a time of international turbulence and economic strain, yet for many, it lacked the boldness and clarity of purpose the electorate felt was needed for the times. For supporters and those who wanted more, the "safe hands" approach that carried him to office was beginning to feel like an albatross around the neck: Australia was yearning for vision, but it received technocratic management instead.

PROLOGUE: THE YEAR OF THE ELECTION

In opposition, Peter Dutton had taken a radically different path and the only path he really knew: division, distortion, and disruption. If Albanese was the steady hand, Dutton was like the rouge security officer with an iron fist and heavy baton—using rhetoric from the interminable culture wars and sharpened by media allies eager to manufacture his self-serving outrage. His campaign had already begun in everything but name, ever since he worked so tirelessly to defeat the Voice to Parliament referendum in 2023. From attacks on renewable energy to unsubstantiated claims of anti-Semitism, from dog-whistling about race and identity to tired slogans about getting Australia "back on track," Dutton's strategy was clear: if he could not inspire, he would inflame and, in the absence of policies, would ride to victory as a five-star general in the culture wars.

But behind the slogans, a greater malaise had taken hold of the country. Australians were *exhausted*—not just from the rising cost of living or the endless housing crisis, but from a political system that seemed incapable of delivering anything beyond slogans, spin, and the superficial. The electorate was no longer just frustrated: it was starting to disengage. The promise of democracy had become more like a procedural contract; the act of voting reduced to choosing between *caution* and *chaos*.

In the distance, the political world itself seemed to be spinning off its axis in the Americas, Europe and the Middle East. Donald Trump had returned to the White House in January, not just as a president but as a messenger of doom and chaos. His second term signalled a new era of global instability—one where alliances were transactional, authoritarianism was fashionable, and democratic norms became more fragile than ever. Australia, long tied to the U.S. through ANZUS and AUKUS, now found itself tied to a crumbling superpower led by a man with no regard for order, law, or truth. And yet, within Canberra, loyalty to Washington remained rock-solid—an article of strategic faith rarely questioned, even as it became increasingly untenable. Would anyone dare talk about this during the campaign?

This was the backdrop to the 2025 federal election: a nation beginning to drift and unsure about its future under a first-term government, a public disillusioned with politics and looking for alternatives to vote for, and a political class unsure of whether to confront the truth or keep performing the same rituals of appeasement and denying the obvious. The challenges were great—housing inequality, Indigenous justice, climate action, economic transformation—but the political responses were too often too small, safe, or just cynical. The Labor government clung to incrementalism as an antidote to failure; the Coalition clung to the past, hoping to reinvent itself as the Howard Government 2.0 and worshipping the gods of international neoliberalism.

As January passed into February, the expected tone of the campaign began to form. The voices grew sharper. The headlines in the mainstream media became nastier. The dividing lines were no longer just about policy—they were about what Australia was, and what it wanted to be. Would it be a country capable of self-reflection and reform, willing to reconcile with its colonial history and economic injustice? Or would it sink deeper into the comfort of cultural denial, animated by flags, empty nationalism, anthems and slogans stripped of meaning?

This federal election—more than many others before it—was a decision-day not just for politicians, but for the nation itself.

PROLOGUE: THE YEAR OF THE ELECTION

A chance to choose *substance* over *spin*. *Unity* over *division*. *Truth* over *fear*. This wasn't an election that would decide everything—elections never serve this purpose—but it would reveal more than the political class was prepared for. And for better or worse, it would tell Australia what kind of country it had become and what it wanted to be in the future.

THE CALM BEFORE THE STORM

December 2024: it was a critical time in federal politics, with the nation geared up for an election that would define the direction of government for the foreseeable future. After months of media-driven speculation about potential election dates in late 2024, the inevitability of a 2025 election was finally realised. That timeline gave the Albanese government a short but critical window to shape the narrative and address the pressing concerns of an electorate already experiencing economic anxieties.

The economy, as always, was front and centre, a reality highlighted by the enduring resonance of former U.S. President Bill Clinton's dictum: *It's the economy, stupid!*—in 2025, this mantra dominated political discourse, just as it had in previous years. Economic issues—interest rates, cost of living, and housing affordability—continued to be the main areas that concerned the electorate, echoing the many unresolved issues of 2024.

The Labor government's management of these issues proved critical, not only to its electoral outcome but also to its credibility as a government that could deliver meaningful change. While the Coalition had eked out a slender lead in the two-party preferred polls at 51 per cent to 49 per cent in December 2024, this margin was far from insurmountable for Labor. Historically, polling that far from an election offers limited predictive value, as voter engagement intensified only once an election was formally called.

Despite the tight polling, the broader political landscape did not suggest an appetite for change: incumbent governments often enjoy structural advantages, and Labor entered the election cycle with a relatively stable platform. However, it had to overcome the reality that it hadn't run a federal campaign from the position of government since 2013—the skills required for campaigning as the incumbent were different from those needed in opposition—and this gap in institutional memory posed some challenges, particularly as election campaigns had become increasingly sophisticated and unpredictable in recent years.

Compounding this challenge was Labor's struggle with political management. While the government had avoided the catastrophic mistakes of the Coalition when it was in government—Scott Morrison's infamous holiday debacle during the national bushfire crisis in 2019 being the most egregious example—its track record was hampered by missed opportunities and a lack of decisiveness. This fed perceptions of a government that was competent but uninspiring—a reputation that proved problematic in the hostile environment of an election campaign. Nevertheless, the Albanese government's stability marked a significant improvement over the tumultuous Coalition governments of recent years, and this steadiness proved enough to hold back voter dissatisfaction.

For the Liberal Party, the road to victory was always perilously narrow. The Leader of the Opposition, Peter Dutton, faced significant hurdles, among them his lack of electoral charisma and appeal in key marginal seats. To overturn Labor's majority and reclaim the heartland Liberal Party seats that were occupied by community independents, the Coalition required an extraordinary effort: a disciplined campaign strategy, a compelling vision for the future, and a leader capable of engaging the electorate on a deeply personal level, qualities that Dutton had yet to demonstrate convincingly. Unless the government's performance in the final months of the campaign deteriorated dramatically, the Coalition's prospects at the election remained slim. However, it was unwise to entirely discount the possibility of a strong opposition campaign, especially given the unpredictable nature of Australian politics.

At that point, Prime Minister Albanese still had the upper hand, but the position for the government was far from unassailable. Labor's ability to capitalise on its incumbency while addressing the electorate's most pressing concerns was the decisive factor in whether it secured a second term.

THE CONTEST OVER AUSTRALIA'S FUTURE AMID ELECTORAL DISCONTENT

Elections are not only a referendum on the past performance of the government; they are battles over the future and which side of politics offered better outcomes for the electorate. While historical precedent favoured first-term governments—all had been re-elected since 1931—the political landscape was always evolving, and no government could rely on these historical precedents. The Albanese government faced the paradox of providing stability—no mean feat when considering the polemical nature of Australian politics since the early

2010s—while contending with deeper vulnerabilities that could be exploited by an opportunist opposition or an increasingly volatile electorate.

One of the Albanese government's potential difficulties lay in its primary vote. Its supporters often pointed to the 2022 election result, where Labor secured 32.6 per cent of the primary vote—the number it held in published opinion polls in late 2024—as proof that the party could hold government with similarly low numbers. However, reliance on historical performance was dangerous. Preference flows under Australia's two-party preferential voting system could swing elections unpredictably, meaning that even an improved primary vote could result in a loss for the Labor government, while a reduced vote could still deliver victory.

This unpredictability highlighted the stakes of the campaign and the importance of coalition-building—both within the Labor base and with other groups such as the Australian Greens, who were publicly alienated by the government throughout much of 2024, primarily over housing policy. Such antagonism risked crucial preference flows, potentially undermining Labor's chances.

Albanese's leadership remained central in this dynamic: while his government had avoided catastrophic governance failures, voter frustration had mounted over perceived inertia on key issues such as housing affordability, climate action, and its lack of interest in international issues such as Palestine, which held significant relevance and resonance within the Australian electorate. Yet, this frustration alone would not equate to electoral defeat. For Albanese, the challenge was less about neutralising dissatisfaction than about presenting a compelling vision for the future—something that required deft political skills and a campaign narrative that inspired trust and optimism.

The Coalition faced its own, arguably greater, challenges. Dutton's polarising persona was both a liability and, paradoxically, a potential asset in certain conservative segments of the electorate. While his hardline positions and lack of broad appeal limited his ability to court swinging voters in marginal urban seats, they resonated with parts of the Coalition's traditional base, particularly in regional and outer-suburban areas.

The Liberal Party's prospects, however, hinged less on Dutton's personal brand and more on the party's ability to craft a coherent message that went beyond just opposing everything proposed by the Labor government. Without a transformative leader or groundbreaking policy agenda, the Coalition risked languishing as an uninspiring alternative to an imperfect government, equipped with nothing more than a megaphone of hostile negativity and a supporting platform provided by the mainstream media.

The Western Australian state election in March provided a crucial bellwether for federal politics. While the extreme dominance of Labor in WA during the 2021 state election was not repeated—winning fifty-three of the fifty-nine seats remains an anomaly—the anticipated natural electoral correction, where the WA Liberal Party picked up seats, did not necessarily signal a broader rejection of Labor at the federal level.

Western Australia's unique political landscape often reflects localised issues rather than federal sentiments, but any significant losses—even if they were part of a natural political correction—emboldened Coalition strategists to target vulnerable federal seats in the state. However, the WA Liberal Party's organisational weakness, with just two lower house seats in the state parliament before the state election in March 2025, complicated its ability to mount a coordinated federal challenge in that state. Albanese's frequent trips to Western Australia over the preceding months suggested an awareness of this delicate balance, as well as the need to reinforce Labor's position in a region where memories of the Coalition's unpopularity still lingered.

Beyond the battleground of Western Australia, the broader electoral map presented additional complications for the Liberal Party. The community independents, who seized a swath of traditionally blue-ribbon Liberal Party seats in 2022, remained entrenched, with high-profile incumbents who continued to enjoy strong community support. These independents, characterised by their alignment with progressive social and environmental policies, effectively neutralised the Liberal Party's hold on affluent urban electorates. The Liberal Party's path back to government required not only recapturing these seats but also holding or gaining ground in regional and suburban battlegrounds—an almost insurmountable task under the circumstances.

THE LEADERSHIP BATTLE BETWEEN ALBANESE AND DUTTON

Leadership undeniably played a defining role throughout 2025, but the state of leadership in Australia's political landscape left much to be desired. Albanese, despite being the incumbent, found himself in a precarious position. While he retained a slight edge as the preferred Prime Minister in opinion polls, his approval ratings had been dragged down to levels similar to those of Dutton. The fact that both leaders held negative net approval ratings at the end of the year reflected a broader dissatisfaction within the electorate—not just with the leaders themselves but with the political system as a whole.

The Albanese government, elected in 2022 with hopes of transformative change, struggled to meet the lofty expectations placed upon it. Many had anticipated a reformist agenda akin to those of the Whitlam or Hawke governments, but instead, the government was characterised by self-imposed incrementalism and an inability to navigate the political battlefield effectively. Its performance in governance was steady, even commendable in many areas, yet its political management was lacklustre. For voters, the disconnect between policy achievements and the government's ability to communicate them effectively fostered a sense of disappointment.

Labor's historical tension between idealism and pragmatism was central to its predicament. The party at times leaned heavily into idealism, as seen in its ambitious climate policies, while neglecting the political groundwork needed to secure public buy-in. In the 1980s and 1990s, figures such as Bob Hawke and Paul Keating mastered the art of balancing these competing forces, crafting a style of leadership that prioritised results while maintaining public support. In contrast, the Albanese government appeared to lack a cohesive political strategy, leaving it vulnerable to criticism and unable to shape the national narrative effectively.

Dutton, for his part, faced even greater leadership hurdles. His divisive politics highlighted a deeper malaise within the Liberal Party, which grappled with declining membership, resource constraints, and an inability to adapt to the shifting political landscape. What became clear, however, was that neither leader had yet articulated a compelling vision for Australia's future. The electorate was not simply searching for competence; it craved direction, purpose, and a sense of optimism. In this regard, both Albanese and Dutton had significant work to do if they hoped to inspire confidence in their leadership.

For Albanese, the path forward lay in reclaiming the narrative and recalling the issues that enabled him to lead the Labor Party to victory in the 2022 federal election. This required not only highlighting his government's policy successes but also demonstrating how these achievements translated into tangible improvements in the lives of Australians. The government had to move beyond the inertia of the past year, presenting a forward-looking agenda that resonated with voters across the spectrum. This meant addressing key issues such as housing affordability, climate action, and economic inequality with both substance and clarity.

Dutton, meanwhile, needed to do much more than simply offer endless criticism of the government; it demanded a positive agenda that appealed to a broader electorate. To that point, Dutton's leadership had been defined more by opposition than proposition, and a seemingly endless culture war against "wokeness"—a strategy that may have galvanised his supporters but fell short of building the kind of leadership needed to win government.

Beyond the leaders themselves, the political system needed to rise to meet the challenges of the moment. Ultimately, the 2025 election was not just a contest between Albanese and Dutton; it was a referendum on the ability of Australia's political leaders and institutions to provide a vision worthy of the nation's future. To succeed, both leaders needed to transcend the narrow confines of political expediency and offer a vision that inspired, united, and addressed the pressing challenges facing Australians. Without this, the election risked being another exercise in managing decline rather than a moment of genuine renewal.

ON TRACK FOR A DIRTY AND DIVISIVE CAMPAIGN

The political year had barely begun, yet the sounds of a federal election were already being loudly heard. Despite January being a month that was usually reserved for rest and reflection, both major political parties had started positioning themselves for the inevitable contest that would eventually be held on May 3. As the stakes rose, so too did the rhetoric, with Peter Dutton charging into the fray—as he usually did—leveraging a mix of typical conservative Liberal Party talking points and calculated distortions to rally his base.

Dutton's soft-launch in Melbourne under the slogan "Let's get Australia back on track" had provided an early glimpse into the Coalition's strategy. While it was better than John Howard's "Incentivation" slogan from the 1987 Liberal Party campaign, what was the track that Dutton wanted Australia to get back to? The long list of incompetence and corruption between 2013 to 2022, when the Coalition was last in office? An economy that was careering towards recession in late 2019 before the Coalition's undeserved economic reputation was rescued by the onset of COVID? Austerity budgets that undermined social cohesion?

Record deficits? Daily division and pitting communities against each other? That track?

The choice of Melbourne—a battleground where the Liberals lost heartland seats to the community independents in 2022—was no accident, and it highlighted their attempts to regain urban and suburban electorates disillusioned with the party's leadership and policies in the past. Yet, the messaging from Dutton revealed very little that was new and was likely to result in the same disillusionment: his attacks on renewable energy, unsubstantiated claims about government complicity in rising anti-Semitism, and promises of lower taxes that history repeatedly disproved, showed a strategy steeped in the politics of fear and division.

Dutton's most inflammatory remark came in the context of anti-Semitism, an issue he pushed with little regard for accuracy or responsibility. He had claimed a staggering 700 per cent surge in anti-Semitism and placed the blame squarely on the Prime Minister's supposed "dereliction of leadership" following protests at the Sydney Opera House after Israel's actions—genocide and ethnic cleansing—commenced in Gaza in October 2023. Such rhetoric was as audacious as it was baseless—the exploitation of deeply sensitive issues for political gain was a tactic as old as politics itself—but its overuse risked alienating an electorate weary of hyperbole and resulted in harmful social division.

Dutton's attempt to resurrect that perennial promise of lower taxes, a pledge that had rarely materialised under previous Coalition governments, also failed: economic data showed that the Howard and Morrison administrations presided over higher tax-to-GDP ratios than many of their predecessors, and taxing levels under Labor governments were consistently lower, undermining the credibility of Dutton's claims. When pressed for specifics, he reverted to that nebulous mantra of "cutting government waste," a trope designed to appeal to fiscal conservatives without committing to meaningful or achievable policy reform.

Dutton's targeting of the public service as "inefficient" was both predictable and disingenuous, ignoring the essential services they provided to the community and the economic stability they supported.

Energy policy was another example of the Coalition's empty rhetoric, with Dutton doubling down on his claim that the government's focus on renewables was undermining Australia's energy security. His assertion that a "renewables-only policy" had caused market uncertainty was a serious oversimplification and a deliberate misrepresentation. Gas continued to play a transitional role in Australia's energy mix—whether people liked it or not—as highlighted by the government's Future Gas Strategy, and Dutton's comments ignored the approach outlined in that very document, an approach that had its antecedents in Coalition policy from when they were last in government. Dutton's framing of renewables as "part-time power" ignored technological advancements in storage and grid stability, pushing a false choice between economic growth and environmental responsibility.

Beneath the surface of Dutton's rhetoric lay a broader strategy: stoke fears of instability and economic decline under Labor's time in government, while offering no alternatives. This was not just political positioning; it was a calculated attempt to shift the narrative, leveraging misinformation to undermine public confidence in the government's ability to manage complex challenges.

However, the contemporary electorate was different to electorates from the past. Australians were more politically engaged, environmentally conscious, and discerning in their assessment of political commentary and claims. The question for Dutton and the Coalition was whether their reliance on old tropes and half-truths would resonate in a landscape where voters were increasingly demanding transparency, accountability, and forward-thinking solutions.

CHOICES IN THE LEADERSHIP FOR AUSTRALIA'S FUTURE

The Prime Minister's response to Dutton's campaign rhetoric was quick, countering the opposition leader's divisive strategies with an alternative vision of unity and progress. The Labor government's slogan, "Building Australia's Future," was a rebuke to Dutton's fear-driven narrative and this response perhaps reflected a broader frustration with this reliance on negative politics and empty promises.

Albanese's response to Dutton's inflammatory claims about anti-Semitism also showed the difference between the two leaders—Dutton's attempt to politicise the deeply sensitive issue of anti-Semitism was met with a measured yet forceful response, in which Albanese detailed the numerous ways he had supported the Jewish community and Israel. While Albanese's support for Palestine had been weak, inadequate, and pathetic, his support for Israel had been unwavering and undeniable—much to the dismay of Palestine's advocates—and aside from Dutton and Zionist lobby groups, who would have preferred Albanese to adopt a stance calling for the complete destruction of Palestine, no one could deny this.

The broader response to Dutton's campaign launch was equally damning, where his launch was characterised as "thirty-eight minutes of empty rhetoric" by members of the Labor government, with no tangible policies offered to alleviate cost-of-living pressures—for a leader attempting to frame himself as a saviour for struggling households, Dutton's failure to present substantive solutions undermined his credibility.

It was easy to critique; it's far harder to constructively contribute, and Dutton's campaign revealed an opposition that remained mired in the politics of negativity. And in an attempt to replicate Donald Trump's proposed Department of Government Efficiency in the U.S., Dutton implied $347 billion in spending cuts that would inevitably target essential services such as pensions, Medicare, and energy bill relief, highlighting the dangerous implications of his rhetoric.

Dutton's vagueness on fiscal policy—deliberately avoiding specifics while gesturing at "government waste," a meaningless mantra if there ever was one—showed a reluctance to confront the real impact of austerity measures. Austerity has failed—as it always does (and more recently in Argentina and New Zealand)—and this lack of transparency left voters questioning what, if anything, the Coalition genuinely stood for beyond opposition to the government of the day.

Albanese, in contrast, had sought to frame his government as a "builder"—focused on creating a future that balanced economic growth with social equity. His emphasis on providing support as something more meaningful than a "sugar hit" revealed a philosophy grounded in long-term nation-building rather than short-term political gains. This perspective, combined with his focus on uniting rather than dividing, directly challenged Dutton's political instincts, which relied heavily on energising a hard-right base rather than appealing to a broader, more inclusive electorate.

Dutton's campaign, at its early stage, appeared to be an exercise in recycling tired conservative talking points: meanwhile, Albanese and his ministers not only called out the emptiness of these talking points but also drew attention to the risks they posed to essential public services and social safety nets. This clear differentiation between the parties—one focused on division and disinformation, the other on unity and pragmatism—became a defining theme as the election approached.

THE ALBANESE–DUTTON CONTEST BETWEEN UNITY AND DIVISION

While it was clear that the 2025 election campaign had essentially already begun at the start of the year, it was also clear that it became defined by personal attacks, manipulative narratives, hollow slogans, and relentless mudslinging—and these conditions proved ripe for what became one of the most bitterly fought federal election campaigns in Australia's history.

Dutton, lacking substantive policies or ideas, dragged the discourse down to his level, resulting in a campaign mired in obfuscation, sludge, and grinding negativity. This strategy created a fog of dirt and confusion, where he had hoped to emerge from the chaos with some kind of victory—and, as expected, he was supported by the mainstream media. It was a disappointing inevitability, but perhaps the greatest tragedy was that it didn't have to be this way.

Albanese entered office with a clear mandate to lead, bolstered by a public eager for stability and progress after nearly a decade of stagnation under successive Coalition governments. In many ways, his government was competent and steady, yet Albanese's determination to seek bipartisanship—particularly from a Liberal Party led by Dutton—diluted his authority and squandered political capital that could have been used to push through transformative policies.

The Voice to Parliament referendum was probably the most obvious example, where Albanese's insistence on securing bipartisan support for what should have been a nation-defining moment of reconciliation and progress allowed Dutton to derail the process, exploiting the opportunity to stoke fear and division. By courting a leader who thrived on wrecking rather than building, Albanese not only weakened his government's position but also deepened the national divide. The referendum's failure remained a wound that lingered well into 2025, and it also served as a warning of the perils of accommodating an opposition that had no interest in genuine collaboration.

On other fronts, Albanese similarly undermined his potential for bold leadership. His government's adherence to the unpopular Stage 3 tax cuts for so long—a relic of a bygone era of Coalition economic policy—baffled both critics and supporters, and when the federal government finally came around to amending this legislation, they received no political benefit.

Why, after nine years in opposition, would a government finally in power sacrifice so much fiscal capacity to uphold a policy that overwhelmingly benefited the wealthy and undermined its broader social agenda? Again, the answer lay in a misguided attempt to avoid alienating right-wing interests and the Coalition, even as Dutton offered nothing in return but contempt and obstruction.

Meanwhile, Dutton capitalised on every misstep and every opportunity given to him—not with vision or policy but with relentless negativity. Like Tony Abbott before him, Dutton was a politician who thrived in opposition, a master of saying "no" but bereft of ideas for governing. His reliance on firebrand rhetoric about "woke" culture, baseless claims about the government's role in societal ills, and constant appeals to conservative fears highlighted his lack of intellectual depth and policy substance. If Abbott's tenure as Prime Minister demonstrated the perils of electing a leader driven by destruction rather than creation, Dutton's would likely have proven even worse. His ambition was not to build a better Australia but to seize power for its own sake.

For Albanese, the 2025 campaign was a critical test. His government had much to campaign on—stability and policy achievements—but these successes were overshadowed by a perception that he had failed to rise to the moment. The spectre of bold, transformative leadership gave way to slow-moving incrementalism that frustrated progressives and emboldened conservatives. Albanese's inability to effectively counter these corrosive tactics from Dutton, and his reluctance to use the crossbench to bypass the Coalition on most occasions, created a contest far closer than it needed to be at that stage of the political cycle.

Unless something dramatic happened in the final stretch of the campaign, the electorate was left with a dilemma: choosing a government that had been competent but timid, or an opposition that was reckless and vacuous. The facile "Let's get Australia back on track" and "Building Australia's future" dominated the campaign trail, but neither slogan captured the disillusionment many Australians felt. In truth, the campaign could be summed up with a sentiment both sobering and aspirational: *Surely Australia Deserves Better.* A better political discourse. A better class of leadership. A better vision for the future. This was what the nation should have demanded from its leaders, yet the unfolding reality suggested it was unlikely to be delivered. Instead, Australians would have to endure a campaign characterised by personal attacks, empty promises, and a sense of frustration with a political system that failed to rise up to the challenges of the modern era. Australia did deserve better—but only if it was prepared to not only ask for it, but to demand it—and it remained up to the community to make those demands.

Political leadership is not just about winning power; it's about using that power to make a difference—and so far, that had not been the case. Certainly, political leadership is difficult and the political rewards are rarely presented easily on a platter—but Albanese was provided with an opportunity to wield power effectively and decided to prioritise bipartisanship with an opposition committed to division, and now risked squandering not only his legacy but also the trust and hope of the Australian people.

For Dutton, the path was simpler but far darker—a campaign of negativity and fear designed to secure power without purpose, much like Tony Abbott's approach in 2013. Ultimately, Australia deserved better than either of these strategies. However, if the early months of 2025 were any indication, it seemed unlikely that anything would change.

UNHAPPY AUSTRALIA DAY AND BLOCKING RECONCILIATION

January 26 once again became the annual circus of cultural and political conflict, and the intent for it to be a "day of national unity" drifted even further out of reach. Instead of collective reflection, the day evolved into social divisions, mainly driven by conservative politicians, media outlets, and their supporting institutions. This transformed January 26, yet again, into a conflict zone within the broader culture wars—a social conflict not searching for resolution, but for constant agitation.

For many in the Indigenous community, January 26 is not a day of celebration but of mourning—a day that signifies colonial dispossession, violence, and the erasure of cultural heritage. *Invasion Day* is a more suitable name, serving as a reminder of the enduring inequalities and injustices faced by First Nations people, even if no federal government has ever officially recognised the day as such.

However, for many other Australians, the day's historical and cultural significance remained nebulous: some associate it with Captain James Cook's landing in 1770; others with the federation of Australia in 1901; and many still see it as nothing more than an opportunity for a public holiday. These varied perceptions reflected a deeper historical amnesia and a lack of consensus about what, if anything, Australia Day is supposed to signify.

The official recognition of January 26 as a national holiday had only been formalised in 1994. Before this, the day was celebrated on different dates, highlighting the absence of a unified national identity around the occasion. Aside from nationalists, there was never universal acceptance or great enthusiasm: here today, gone tomorrow and forgotten. Instead, the day became increasingly polarised, with figures like Peter Dutton and the Murdoch media wielding it as a rhetorical weapon in a broader ideological struggle that few outside their base care about.

Dutton's rhetoric about Australia Day being a "day of shame" for those who refused to celebrate it—despite millions taking to the streets across Australia in protest—revealed no genuine concern for national unity. Dutton even refused to attend Australia Day events in Canberra. His aim was a calculated attempt to inflame division for political gain. Not to be outdone by her leader's absurdity, Sussan Ley compared the arrival of the First Fleet to Elon Musk's space missions to Mars, claiming that it was "not an invasion," nor even an intention to destroy or pillage—even though that was precisely what the First Fleet did in 1788.

This weaponised version of January 26 formed part of a larger conservative project to entrench cultural narratives prioritising uncritical patriotism and historical whitewashing. For Dutton, the day represented an opportunity to rally his base against perceived threats to Australian identity, whether those threats were supermarket chains choosing not to stock Australia Day merchandise or vague claims of people being "afraid to celebrate".

But who, exactly, was afraid? Where were these people? What were they supposedly afraid of?

These grievances—often manufactured or exaggerated—serve as distractions from the substantial issues facing the nation. They allow conservatives to frame themselves as defenders of "tradition" and "national pride" while avoiding meaningful engagement with the historical and ongoing injustices experienced by Indigenous Australians.

The insistence on treating January 26 only as a joyous occasion, festooned with balloons, streamers, flags, barbecues, and beach parties, demonstrates a refusal to understand or engage with the complexities of Australia's history. Dutton indulged in a childlike fantasy—a superficial celebration that ignored the deeper wounds and contradictions embedded in the nation's history. This approach was not only insensitive but counterproductive. By insisting on uncritical celebration, conservatives alienated large segments of the population who wanted to use the day as an opportunity for reflection, dialogue, and acknowledgment of historical wrongs. In doing so, they perpetuated the very divisions they claimed to oppose.

The Prime Minister's framing of Australia Day as an "opportunity to celebrate everything we've built together" and to be "optimistic for the future" struck a more conciliatory tone but still fell short of addressing the underlying tensions. While optimism and unity are admirable aspirations, they could not be achieved without confronting the darker chapters of Australia's history and the structural inequalities that still persist. For many, the gap between the idealised and saccharine vision of Australia

Day and the lived realities of the marginalised and excluded made the celebration hollow—if not offensive.

The shame and division conservatives claimed to oppose did not come from public opposition to the day itself but from their own efforts to enforce a singular, exclusionary narrative about its meaning. Their fixation on cultural grievances—whether over supermarket shelves or imagined fears of celebration—reflect an unwillingness to engage in the difficult but necessary work of national Reconciliation. Until this work is undertaken, January 26 remains a contested symbol, emblematic not of unity but of the unresolved conflicts at the centre of the Australian identity.

A CONTESTED LEGACY OF DIVISION AND HISTORICAL AMNESIA

For Indigenous Australians, January 26 marks a devastating part of their history. The arrival of the First Fleet in 1788 brought the imposition of British law, the seizure of land under the doctrine of *terra nullius*—in direct contradiction to King George's instructions to Governor Phillip—and the systematic destruction of Indigenous cultures over time. Resistance, often painted by conservatives as a modern phenomenon, was deeply rooted in Australian history: as early as 1938, the Day of Mourning drew attention to the injustices that January 26 represented.

Despite the historical inaccuracy and insensitivity of the 1938 reenactments of the First Fleet's landing and encounters with Indigenous people, the events at least recognised that the Australia Day narrative was incomplete and exclusionary. These protests were not isolated, but part of a continuum of resistance: the Bicentenary events of 1988—thirty-seven years ago—saw over 40,000 Indigenous and non-Indigenous people march through Sydney in solidarity. They condemned the ongoing injustices faced by Aboriginal communities and demanded recognition of their rights. That moment helped embed the idea of 'Invasion Day' in the national consciousness and highlighted the need for a more inclusive and honest understanding of Australia's history.

Despite Australia Day historically being celebrated in May, June or July, conservative forces became entrenched in their opposition to changing the date. This refusal reflects a broader trend of uncritical nationalism, which—as seen in other countries—has proved to be deeply corrosive. Rooted in hollow symbols like the flag and the national anthem, this brand of nationalism thrives on superficial pride, detached from the historical and social complexities that shaped the nation. Australia Day perpetuates a sanitised version of history that ignores the violence and dispossession that modern Australia was built upon.

A SYMBOLIC DISTRACTION PUSHED BY CONSERVATIVES

The conservative obsession with Australia Day and their confected outrage over any challenge to its format revealed a deeper truth—this was never about the date or even national pride: it was about controlling the national narrative and resisting uncomfortable truths. For decades, January 26 had been an innocuous date for many non-Indigenous Australians, more about leisure than historical reflection—largely because few knew its true significance. Its transformation into a conservative rallying point was not driven by widespread sentiment but by a calculated political strategy: to weaponise cultural issues and sow division for electoral gain.

Dutton thrived on this cycle of outrage. He manufactured crises over "woke culture," accused opponents of stoking division, and relied on a compliant media to amplify the story. True to form, that was exactly what happened in 2023. The Voice to Parliament referendum illustrated this perfectly: a modest, practical proposal to enshrine an Indigenous advisory body in the Constitution was crushed under waves of racist misinformation and fearmongering. It failed not because the idea lacked merit, but because conservatives sowed confusion and resentment. Albanese's efforts—though well-intentioned and poorly executed—were reframed as part of an "elite agenda," with political consequences that lingered well into the 2025 election.

This cycle was not limited to the Voice or Australia Day. It was part of a broader "Trumpist" playbook—symbolic battles in place of policy solutions. These tactics worked in 2023 because they exploited fear: fear of change, of losing control, of confronting history. For leaders like Dutton, sustaining that fear was essential, allowing them to pose as defenders of tradition while actively resisting progress.

Changing the date of Australia Day would have been symbolic—but what Australia needs is a transformation in its attitudes towards Indigenous people and its colonial legacy. That work remains massive, made harder by conservative denialism and childish rhetoric. Their fantasies about an idealised, untroubled past erased Indigenous voices and realities. It's an ongoing fiction that prevents the country from moving forward.

Perhaps it is time to cede January 26 to the conservatives—to let them celebrate their symbolic victories and exhaust themselves with outrage and performative patriotism. Progressives could then redirect focus onto real issues—pathways to justice and genuine Reconciliation. A Treaty with Indigenous people, for example, has never required a referendum or the consent of the conservative Stasi. If the Liberal Party—and the easily manipulated—chose agitation over progress, so be it. Those with courage and will can move forward without them. Initiatives such as the First Peoples' Assembly in Victoria and the Noongar Settlement in Western Australia have proved that meaningful action didn't need fanfare or national division.

The fight over Australia Day will always be a distraction—one that conservatives refuse to relinquish: it serves their brand of politics too well. But progressives face a choice: remain in this ritualised culture war, or bypass it entirely and deliver meaningful change. The path to justice will always be difficult—and clearly, it will not be cleared by those who profited from the obstacles. Maybe now is the time to finally leave January 26 behind—and define the future by the real work of Reconciliation, not the confected outrage of those who opposed it.

THE CHAOS AND UNRAVELLING OF AN AMERICAN DEMOCRACY

By early February, Donald Trump was the president of the United States for a second term and, after the events of 2021 at the Capitol Hill riots—amongst many other incidents during his first term—this defied political logic but, as the Americans like to say, *it is what it is*. The echoes of the chaos of 2017 had returned, except this time, the chaos was deliberate, premeditated, and unrestrained by the checks and balances that once tempered Trump's first presidency.

The opening days of his return to power were filled with the same erratic grandstanding that had defined his first term: ridiculous territorial demands, aggressive posturing on the world stage, and a calculated descent into authoritarian theatrics. In just the first week, he threatened to seize the Panama Canal, issued a demand to annex Greenland from Denmark, and renamed the Gulf of Mexico as the Gulf of America.

But the United States couldn't just seize the Panama Canal: it's sovereign territory, and any attempt to seize it would have been an act of war. Greenland has been under Danish sovereignty for over two centuries: it couldn't just be handed over to the United States, despite what Trump said.

These demands were ridiculous at face value but that was precisely the point. They provoked outrage, confusion, and endless media speculation: was Trump serious? Could the U.S. military actually be deployed to seize foreign lands at his command? Could he do this? The moment was reminiscent of the early days of his first presidency when he blustered about NATO, threatened nuclear war with North Korea, and fired cabinet members over Twitter. It was chaos as a strategy, a deliberate means to exhaust opposition, saturate the media cycle, and prevent the public from focusing on his real agenda of extremism.

Trump made moves that had profound and lasting consequences for the fabric of American society—behind the smokescreen of his global provocations, he systematically dismantled civil rights, and his administration began its rollback of women's reproductive rights with unprecedented speed.

LGBTQ+ protections, already eroded in his first term, were now actively dismantled, with federal agencies ordered to purge diversity initiatives and inclusion programs. His government rapidly moved toward the wholesale disenfranchisement of marginalised communities, curtailing voting rights through gerrymandering, state suppression laws, and judicial manipulation.

He stacked his administration with loyalists who were not just corrupt but ideologically extreme, openly espousing white nationalist rhetoric and religious fundamentalism. The Republican Party, having purged itself of dissenters in the wake of Trump's return, acted as a rubber stamp, enabling his most draconian policies without resistance.

This corruption was brazen: positions of authority were handed out to unqualified loyalists, many of whom had open criminal records (including Trump) or ties to extremist groups. Government agencies were stripped of career professionals and replaced with sycophants whose only qualification was their unwavering sycophancy to Trump.

Regulations were slashed, environmental protections removed, corporate oligarchs given free rein to exploit the economy—America, already teetering on the edge of political and economic instability, entered an era of unrestricted corruption. But despite this, even more alarming was the escalation of Trump's authoritarian ambitions and fascist tendencies.

He began floating plans to round up undocumented immigrants and place them in mass detention centres, with Guantanamo Bay openly discussed as a primary holding facility. The administration's rhetoric shifted from coded language to open calls for mass deportations and state-sanctioned crackdowns. The imagery was familiar, in a historical parallel too obvious to ignore. This wasn't simply about enforcement—it was about intimidation, fear, and the normalisation of state-sponsored persecution. And we didn't have to worry about revisiting historical clichés or invoking Godwin's law of Nazi analogies: this was brutal fascism, and we weren't afraid to call it out, from wherever we were.

Trump's legal battles, which once seemed like they might prevent his return to power, appeared almost as a footnote of history. The

Supreme Court, packed with his handpicked judges, provided legal cover for his most extreme policies. The Constitution, once an obstacle to his ambitions, was now little more than a suggestion. Executive orders and legal loopholes were exploited to strip citizenship from those deemed politically undesirable. And, as usual, there were many contradictions—many of Trump's closest allies, including his new head of Department of Government Efficiency, Elon Musk, and even his own wife, Melania Trump, benefited from the very immigration policies he now sought to dismantle. Double standards were no longer a liability in Trump's America; it was a feature of the system he built.

However, despite this unprecedented power grab, there were pockets of resistance: Trump's hold on the federal government was strong, but states with Democratic leadership began to fight back. Legal challenges mounted, with governors refusing to comply with federal directives, and sanctuary cities dug in their heels against mass deportation efforts. The battle lines were seemingly drawn, and the coming months determined whether the United States remained a functioning democracy or fully descended into authoritarian rule. The question was no longer whether Trump would push America toward decline; it was whether anyone could stop him before it was too late.

AN OPPORTUNITY TO BREAK FREE FROM AMERICA'S DECLINE

The farcical nature of United States politics had long been a source of derision—for outsiders—even when the Democrats held power, but under Trump's second presidency, it escalated from dysfunction to something far more dangerous. And it was dangerous, there was no question about this. And this danger—albeit from a faraway distance—would feature prominently in Australia's election.

The U.S. is still, for now, the world's most powerful and influential nation, but it is slipping, not only because of Trump, but because of a long-term decline brought on by political instability, economic stagnation, and strategic miscalculations, concurrent with the rise of China, which will soon overtake the U.S, militarily and economically. While most of the world watched in despair as Trump took the sledgehammer and angle grinder to democratic norms, Australia was faced with an unavoidable question: Should it continue tying its fortunes to a crumbling and increasingly dysfunctional superpower, or should it grab the opportunity to establish itself as an independent, strategically autonomous nation with new and diversified alliances?

The spectacle of Trump's leadership—an erratic and bombastic return to authoritarian populism, as well as behaving like America's *arsehole-in-chief*—may have seemed like a uniquely American phenomenon, but there were serious implications for Australia. His first term was a warning sign; his second term was where the results of his reckless ideology would come to fruition. The "idiot king" model of politics, the elevation of incompetence as a virtue, the aggressive use of chaos to mask deeper, more insidious policy shifts—these weren't just the problems of the United States, but were symptoms of a political virus that had infected democracies worldwide.

History had seen this before: Mussolini in Italy, Hitler's weaponisation of grievance politics in Germany—leaders who turned democracy into a circus before transforming it into something far more sinister and disastrous. This history was being repeated, and no country that considered itself an ally of the United States could afford to ignore what this shift meant for the future.

Australia had long been tethered to American strategic interests, often at the expense of its own. The ANZUS alliance, the AUKUS agreement, the constant diplomatic and military alignment—these were framed as necessities, but in truth, they left Australia vulnerable to the chaos of the American decline. Trump's second term was an opportunity, maybe even a final warning, that Australia must reassess its place in the world. Blind loyalty to the United States, especially through AUKUS, no longer served Australian interests. Instead, Australia needed to forge new and better relationships—ones that reflects its geographic reality and its economic priorities, rather than outdated Cold War allegiances that were now liabilities.

China, despite the diplomatic strain of recent years, remained Australia's largest trading partner by a significant margin. Under the Albanese government, tensions eased, but the deeper question remained: why should Australia continue preparing for military confrontation with a nation it was so economically dependent on?

The AUKUS agreement, sold to the public as a necessary counter to Chinese influence, served British and American interests far more than it served Australia's. The nuclear submarines promised under AUKUS were unlikely to arrive in any meaningful capacity for decades, and even if they did, they served more as an extension of U.S. military power in the Pacific than as an asset to Australian defences. The cost—both financial and geopolitical—was enormous, and it locked Australia into an American strategic framework that assumed perpetual hostility with China. But what if that assumption was wrong? What if Australia's best path forward wasn't through military escalation but through deeper economic and diplomatic integration with its regional neighbours?

Indonesia, India, and the broader south-east Asian region represented an alternative vision for Australian foreign policy—one based on pragmatism rather than ideological servitude to Washington. Indonesia, a rapidly growing economic power with deep historical trade ties to Australia, should have been a priority partner, yet it was often treated as an afterthought in Australian diplomacy, as though our nearest neighbour with a population of over 270 million simply didn't exist.

India, now the world's most populous democracy and a rising global power, offered another key strategic relationship that could have been cultivated independently of American influence. The Keating-era view of Asia as Australia's "near north" remained just as true in 2025 as it was in the 1990s. A future-oriented Australian foreign policy recognised that its long-term security did not lie in being America's proxy in an imaginary Pacific Cold War, but in fostering strong, independent partnerships with the nations that would define the region's economic and political future.

This didn't mean severing ties with the United States entirely: Australia's relationship with the U.S. was deep, and there were areas of mutual benefit that should not be abandoned. But the blind allegiance, the kind that dragged Australia into unnecessary military conflicts, the kind that forced it to take economic hits due to American-led trade disputes, the kind that undermined its own regional credibility—that needed to end. Australia did not need to choose between America and China, or between old alliances and new ones, in the same way it didn't need to end the relationship with Britain when it veered towards the U.S. after World War II. It needed to assert its own national interests, something it had failed to do for decades due to the sphere of American influence.

History shows that global power shifts moves at a glacial pace and doesn't happen overnight, but they are happening. America's decline wasn't immediate, nor was China's rise without complications. But Australia couldn't afford to wait: it needed to act to establish itself as a nation with independent strategic capabilities and diversified alliances. The U.S. under Trump was a reminder that tying Australia's fate too closely to a declining empire was a dangerous gamble: its future is in the Indo–Pacific region, not in the ashes of American exceptionalism.

It was no longer a question of whether Australia should begin this transition—it was a question whether it had the political will to do this before it was too late. The Albanese government could have dumped the AUKUS deal when it first came to office in 2022 but decided not to. It took some steps to repair relations with China and deepen engagement with south-east Asia, but the broader shift required was one that would take a lot more political courage.

It meant questioning deeply entrenched assumptions about Australia's place in the world and resisting the pressure from Washington to remain in lockstep with American military priorities. It also meant acknowledging the fact that the world was changing and Australia needed to take the crucial steps to change with it.

Trump's second term was a test for American democracy but it was also a test to see if Australia could finally break free from the outdated mindset that kept it languishing in America's shadow for far too long. Australia needed to decide whether it would move in synch with a changing world or be left behind, clinging to alliances that no longer served its interests.

THE DESCENT INTO TRUMPISM AND THE FAILURE TO FIGHT BACK

The Liberal Party in Australia has never been a stranger to opportunism but under Peter Dutton, it fully embraced the Trumpist model of lies, division, and performative outrage. Despite media attempts to frame Dutton as "different" to Donald Trump's brand of chaotic politics—the ABC editorialised that Dutton was "unlikely to read from Trump's playbook as the election neared"—the evidence spoke for itself.

The culture wars, the shameless populism, the deliberate misinformation and disinformation—all of this followed the same blueprint that worked so effectively for right-wing populists across the world, including Trump. The appointment of Jacinta Price as the spokesperson for government efficiency was a perfect example, mirroring Trump's own hollow attempt at "government efficiency," a meaningless title that masked the real intent: dismantling public institutions while enriching corporate interests under the guise of cutting bureaucratic "waste," as early indications from Elon Musk's actions in the U.S. suggested. The hypocrisy was pretty obvious—Dutton and

Price, along with other Liberal Party figures, had been among the most egregious abusers of taxpayer-funded luxuries.

Price spent $76,000 on business class flights during the Voice to Parliament referendum in 2023, $21,000 on a flight to attend a cost-of-living committee meeting. Dutton also spent $23,000 for flights to a Gina Rinehart-sponsored Bush Summit, $63,000 for himself and his staff members to fly to another cost-of-living meeting, and $6,000 to attend Rinehart's social gathering in Western Australia. Excellent examples of wasteful largesse.

And on top of this, there was the wastefulness and corruption from during the Coalition's time in office between 2013 to 2022. But hypocrisy didn't seem to matter in this era of conservative politics: the only thing that mattered was controlling the narrative, and the right has mastered this art.

Despite the clear and evident failures of Trump between 2017–21, Boris Johnson in the UK, and Scott Morrison in Australia, right-wing populism was still thriving, as if the electorate formed a collective amnesia about these experiences, and the expectation that this incompetence would lead to a broad rejection of their politics proved to be false. Instead, they were replaced by a new generation of populist leaders who learned from their mistakes—Dutton refined the formula: avoid Trump's excesses but maintain his tactics, weaponise cultural division, and manufacture outrage while simultaneously promising to gut public services.

This persistence of right-wing populism was not just a reflection of the weakness of its opponents—it was a sign of a deeper ideological failure on the part of centrist and centre-left politics.

Leaders such as Joe Biden, Keir Starmer and Anthony Albanese did not fail in governance on the face of it; they had, for the most part, restored basic competence and stability after the chaos of their predecessors. But within their political strategies and in the "game" of politics, they had been inadequate.

The response to right-wing populism was weak, defensive, and uninspiring, especially in the case of Albanese, who did promise a "careful and cautious government," and delivered that in spades, just at a time where a bolder direction was needed and demanded from the electorate. But in trying to be sensible and moderate, they ceded the political battlefield to the extremists. Biden in the U.S. resembled a cadaver-like figure, easily opened to ridicule. Starmer in the UK had a different set of problems, but suffered drastically by being a massive do-nothing disappointment, despite the massive victory the electorate gave him at the 2024 general election.

Albanese ceded so much ground to his opponent—and some of this could be sheeted home to the mainstream media and its relentless promotion of Dutton—some, but not all. If Albanese had a more compelling narrative to provide to the media and the electorate, and just been a little bit more interesting, and true to himself, he wouldn't have had the Labor government in a position where, based on current opinion polling, their best outcome at the federal election was a barely manageable minority government.

The failure of the left to counteract right-wing populism stemmed from an unwillingness to confront the big ideological con at the heart of modern politics: neoliberalism. The economic order that dominated the West since the 1980s—built on privatisation, deregulation, and the gutting of the welfare state—created the perfect conditions for right-wing populism to thrive. Yet the supposed opponents of this order, the centre-left parties, not only failed to dismantle it, but in many cases, actively participated in its expansion. Tony Blair in the UK; Bill Clinton in the U.S.; Bob Hawke and Paul Keating locally; they may have implemented some progressive social policies, but they also embraced the neoliberal economic model, locking in a system that prioritised corporate interests over public welfare.

This was the real reason why centre-left parties struggled to counteract figures like Dutton and Trump—they refuse to challenge the economic structures that created the conditions for right-wing populism in the first place. Centrist and centre-left politics talk about fighting inequality—such as Albanese's "no one left behind"—but refuse to abandon the policies that sustained it.

Instead of presenting a clear alternative, they offer minor adjustments to an economic system that had already failed millions. Meanwhile, the right exploit the discontent this system generated—even though they were the ones who created and promoted this system in the early 1980s—redirecting public anger away from the real sources of their hardship and towards convenient scapegoats: immigrants, minorities, the "woke elite". Margaret Thatcher and Ronald Reagan would have been proud of their handiwork.

The neoliberal con is everywhere in Australia today. Private health insurance is a racket that does little more than shift public money into corporate hands. Private education is a status symbol that offers no real academic advantage over the public system, yet receives disproportionate government funding. Private infrastructure contracts routinely cost more than public projects, yet the government continues to outsource essential services to private firms which prioritised profits over efficiency. Even the media landscape has been distorted by neoliberal logic, with public broadcasters such as the ABC increasingly compromised by the influence of corporate interests and the fear of offending anyone.

The only way to break this cycle is for centre-left politics to abandon its timidity and reassert a bold vision for government, starting with high-level economic reform. The great reformers of history—whether from the left or the right—didn't succeed by cautiously hedging their bets: they succeeded by taking clear, decisive stands. Thatcher in the UK; John Howard in Australia: for all their faults, they never wavered in their ideological convictions. Their policies were disastrous for working people, but they pursued their ideological intentions, despite how despicable they were.

In contrast, too many modern centre-left leaders were afraid to challenge the status quo in any meaningful way, even though implementing a true centre-left political and economic agenda would have appeased the people who intended to vote against them. If only they had the courage and foresight to understand what the correlation is...

There needs to be a starting point to weaken the influence of corporate and vested interests and restoring government control over essential services—healthcare, education, infrastructure—would remove some of the worst distortions created by privatisation. A more progressive taxation system, with aggressive measures to crack down on corporate tax avoidance, could help fund these initiatives without relying on endless budget cuts.

Of course, any government—which would typically have been a centre-left government—that pursued such reforms would have faced a brutal backlash. The media, heavily aligned with corporate interests, would have painted them as radical extremists, and the business elite would have done everything in their power to discredit them. And yet, this is exactly what is required.

The reason right-wing populists have been so successful is that they are willing to play dirty politics, take the risks, to reshape political discourse in their favour. The centre-left has to be willing to do the same—not by embracing dishonesty and division, but by refusing to play by the rigged rules of neoliberalism and changing the system in their favour. This was what conservatives have done whenever they are in office, so why can't progressive parties do the same?

Australia had one of the best electoral systems in the world, and compulsory voting prevents the voter suppression that has become rampant in many parts of the United States. But the voter apathy remains, with that prevailing sentiment that "both sides are the same," because, in too many ways, it is true.

If centre-left parties—or those masquerading as centre-left—continued to just manage neoliberalism rather than dismantle it, then they will continue to lose the political war. The populists keep winning, not because they have better policies, but because they offered something clear, something emotionally compelling, something that speaks to the frustrations of people who feel abandoned by the political system, even though these populists offered no solutions and actually promise to offer more punishment to the people affected by their policies.

The question wasn't whether left (or left-ish) parties can win elections—Albanese, Biden, and Starmer already proved that they can. The question is whether they could do anything meaningful with their victories and, so far, they haven't. If they continue to play it safe, if they continue to avoid confronting the fundamental flaws of the economic system, then their time in power could be brief.

The next wave of right-wing populists are always waiting, ready to exploit every failure, every disappointment, every instance of inaction, and then offer more of the same. And if that happens, the next Trump or Dutton wouldn't just be an opportunistic populist—they would be something far worse, as we had already started to see in the United States.

ALBANESE'S GAMBLE ON U.S. TARIFFS

By mid-February, the imposition of a 25 per cent tariff on steel and aluminium imports into the United States had become an important political issue, not just for the Australian government, but many governments around the world. The phone call made by Prime Minister Anthony Albanese to President Donald Trump was the start of an attempt to secure exemptions from the tariff, and although the volume of steel and aluminium exports that Australia sent to the United States was relatively small, the political ramifications of being denied an exemption were great. In an election year, Albanese couldn't afford to look ineffective when managing Australia's relationship with the United States, one of its most important strategic and economic partners.

Australia exports around 10 per cent of its overall steel and aluminium to the United States: around $638 million in steel and $275 million in aluminium. While that figure wasn't a dominant share of Australian exports in those sectors, there was a symbolic importance of securing an exemption. Trade with the United States had historically been weighted in favour of the U.S., a point Albanese emphasised during the phone call to Trump—a relatively unique position given the then-current U.S. approach to global trade—and in response, Trump described Albanese as a "very fine man" and acknowledged that the United States had "one of the few" trade surpluses with Australia, but his promise to give Australia's request "great consideration" remained vague.

The political implications for Albanese were tied to how the Coalition and the mainstream media would interpret a failure to secure an exemption—their responses were predictably negative—and with a federal election due soon, this was precisely the time when incumbent leaders looked to strengthen their standings with policy or diplomatic successes. Failing to secure an agreement provided fertile ground for his political adversaries, opening the Prime Minister to criticisms that he couldn't manage the U.S.–Australia relationship.

There was also the broader challenge posed by the unpredictability of President Trump's style of governing, if that's what it could have been called. His decisions often appeared more reactive than strategic, and seemed to arise from immediate calculations of what might have been most politically advantageous to him or to his political MAGA base.

The expectation of results based on rules, longstanding alliances, and careful consultation no longer applied under this President, who was willing to announce or retract sweeping economic policies at whim, and this impulsiveness made negotiating an exemption fraught with uncertainty: one day, an exemption might have been promised or hinted at; the next, a change in the President's mood or priorities could have jeopardised that entire arrangement.

TRUMP'S MINDSET AND THE IMPACT ON AUSTRALIA

Trump's unpredictability—and the purpose behind this unpredictability—remained the main difficulty for any government attempting to navigate these tariffs, not just Australia. The other consideration was that it was not clear if the stated policy goal of bolstering American steel and aluminium production was achievable in a straightforward way—building new or reviving disused smelters in the United States was a long process that might have taken twelve months or more, during which time shortages could have led to increased prices for American manufacturers. This outcome would have contradicted Trump's broader political ambitions for reduced costs and stronger domestic industries, as well as complicated other trade areas, as unpredictability in one policy area could have leaked into others, potentially prompting more tariffs or retaliatory measures on other products.

From an Australian perspective, the biggest concern was the hit taken by domestic exporters who relied heavily on the United States market. For companies sending the majority of their goods to America, a 25 per cent tariff would have made them uncompetitive unless they could quickly find alternative markets. However, as seen in the disrupted trade with China caused by former prime minister Scott Morrison and Peter Dutton in 2020, repositioning to new markets was rarely quick or painless. The complex web of global commerce meant exporters needed stable, predictable trading environments to manage supply chains and plan for the future. When major partners installed sudden barriers, even a moderate drop in export volumes could have cascaded through entire industries.

Trump's style also highlighted how different he was from his predecessors who, even if controversial in their policy decisions—such as George W. Bush—tended to operate within a more defined framework of institutional checks and long-term strategic thinking. For all of his failings, Bush at least listened to a cross-section of quality advisers and recognised the importance of ongoing alliances. In contrast, Trump's style was more theatrical and capricious, leveraging unpredictability in an attempt to extract concessions.

Yet this kind of brinkmanship could also have backfired: Mexico and Canada demonstrated that standing firm did not always result in worse terms. Trump ended up settling for essentially the same deals with these countries that already existed, loudly declaring victory in an arrangement that scarcely changed from the previous framework. This pattern suggested that Trump thrived on conflict to project strength, even when the outcomes remained unchanged. In practical terms, that meant Australia's best strategy may well have been to remain steadfast, continue negotiations, and present a clear-eyed view of the mutual benefits that came from open markets—but also understanding that final decisions could have hinged on a whim, an impulse, or a fleeting political calculation by Trump.

All of this made the environment precarious for trade partners such as Australia. Just as trade could help maintain positive relationships between countries, it could also become a weapon wielded by leaders who saw diplomatic norms as inconveniences that could be easily discarded. While it might have been tempting to ignore the theatrics and histrionics of the White House, the potential damage to export industries—and to Prime Minister Albanese's political standing—couldn't be so easily dismissed.

RETHINKING AUSTRALIA'S SUBSERVIENCE TO THE UNITED STATES

Australia's deep alignment with the United States had long been anchored in shared post-war interests spanning trade, defence, intelligence, and broader geopolitical objectives. Successive governments in Canberra reinforced these bonds through significant policy commitments and major defence arrangements, sometimes at substantial financial cost with little direct reciprocal benefit beyond broad declarations of "strong" partnerships and media opportunities for political leaders. Decisions such as the AUKUS payment of $US500 million facilitated by Defence Minister Richard Marles showed how concessions—and payments—were consistently provided in the hope of preserving good relations and avoiding any appearance of disloyalty. In many ways, this dynamic was reminiscent of the presentation of tributes and gifts to medieval rulers—gold, jewellery or exotic animals—offered more out of obsequious obligation and fear of disfavour than from a balanced negotiation between equals.

The dilemma was not that Australia should seek to jettison its alliance with the United States; the strategic value was somewhat clear, and there was little appetite to unravel decades of cooperation between the two countries. The question was whether Australian leaders should have been more steadfast in articulating national interests, rather than kowtowing to the United States. Time and again, Canberra matched or even surpassed Washington's requests, whether by allocating funds, supporting military interventions, or echoing foreign policy positions, especially in the Middle East. In return, direct practical benefits were elusive. This pattern of behaviour suggested that while the alliance's ideological relationship remained strong—rooted in democratic values and a shared history—a default position of unquestioning support placed Australia on the back foot whenever disputes arose.

The example of New Zealand in the 1980s was important in this context, when they were suspended from the ANZUS Treaty over visiting rights for nuclear-powered ships and submarines—in 1984, NZ Prime Minister David Lange enacted legislation to keep New Zealand a nuclear-free zone—and this incident showed that a smaller country could maintain a strong relationship with the United States and its allies, yet still carve out policies that reflected domestic priorities and strategic judgments.

By acting with a measure of independent resolve, New Zealand managed to reinforce its sovereignty—and national dignity—without irreparably damaging trade or relationships with the United States. Australia could have adopted a similar stance, promoting the alliance when it aligned with national objectives but drawing clearer lines when pressured to make concessions of dubious benefit, which was what AUKUS essentially was.

The concern, of course, was that Trump—already known for taking perceived slights personally—might have retaliated by imposing or refusing to remove tariffs, just because he didn't like Albanese. Or for comments made by Kevin Rudd. Or Scott Morrison. Or for some other spurious reason. Yet that risk was not a permanent condition, and even within the United States, political support for Trump's combative approach was far from unanimous. Tying national interests too tightly to the impulses of one individual—albeit the President of the United States—could have hampered longer-term strategic thinking, especially given the shifting nature of contemporary American politics. A leadership that was consistently ready to meet every whim with acquiescence risked undervaluing its own bargaining position and squandering the chance to negotiate more durable outcomes.

A recalibrated Australian foreign policy didn't need to reject a longstanding ally. Instead, it would have reflected a clear-eyed understanding that large powers acted primarily in their own interests, no matter what type of assurances of friendship were provided. If securing an exemption from the steel and aluminium tariffs became purely transactional—as it undoubtedly did—Australia should have felt entitled to drive a harder bargain and this might even have earned greater respect in the long term. The reflexive deference then on display, however, suggested an unbalanced relationship that would have continued to exact a price unless Australia chose to govern its affairs with the same conviction it had often shown in other facets of its global engagement.

AUSTRALIA KEEPS FAILING TO CLOSE THE GAP

The *Closing the Gap* report continued to expose the disadvantages faced by Aboriginal and Torres Strait Islander peoples, yet it didn't generated the urgent, comprehensive action that was required to address them. Since the first report was tabled in 2008, governments of all persuasions have presented variations of pretty much the same report year after year, but failed to deliver even the minimal shifts required to make substantial changes.

In this latest report, of the nineteen socio-economic targets identified for improvement by 2031, only five were on track. *Five.* There was progress in ensuring more Indigenous children accessed early childhood education, in boosting healthy weight outcomes for newborns, and in transferring legal control of more land and sea country back to Aboriginal and Torres Strait Islander custodians—these were significant benchmarks, and they highlighted that positive change was possible where strategic commitments received focused investment and community-led engagement.

Yet these improvements were counteracted by worsening outcomes in other critical areas. The life expectancy gap remained stubbornly high, incarceration rates for Indigenous Australians continued to climb, and suicide rates not only failed to decrease but were in fact escalating. More broadly, the various forms of disadvantage within education, housing, health, and employment continued to reflect deep inequities that had evolved after centuries of dispossession and discrimination.

Each year this report surfaced, it highlighted how structural factors continued to entrench poverty, lack of opportunity, and social marginalisation. Meanwhile, the frustrations grew louder for Indigenous people: too many policymakers appeared happy with small, piecemeal efforts that did not alter the foundations of inequality. When resistance to increased funding or support appeared—often from the right-wing voices that questioned why Indigenous communities deserved "special" treatment—the bigger historical and social picture was ignored, as if centuries of exclusion could be overturned by the barest minimum of resources.

What the data revealed was that these gaps persisted not just because of any single misstep by a government agency or the personal choices of individuals, but because of a wide-scale failure to address the root causes. It was simplistic to assume that higher rates of incarceration were just a reflection of more crime, without considering how intergenerational trauma, continued marginalisation, and cultural alienation drove certain actions in the first place.

It was equally narrow-minded to say that increased funding had been misspent or wasted, without looking at why communities were forced to operate under resource stress and constant policy churn. Year after year, such simplistic narratives derailed meaningful debates, shifted blame around rather than seeking more meaningful and longer-term solutions. Meanwhile, the gap remained wide, a national shame that intensified every year these statistics were released. Rather than accepting another repetitive cycle in which largely the same report was presented with little tangible progress, a complete transformation in approach was needed—one that went beyond small and cosmetic changes, and instead looked into the structural realities that kept Indigenous peoples at a disadvantage.

THE TOP-DOWN APPROACH KEEPS FAILING

Despite decades of evidence that a strictly top-down approach produces disappointing outcomes, governments continue to dictate the terms of Indigenous affairs rather than meaningfully partner with communities. Large funding announcements have been made—such as the $842 million earmarked for the Northern Territory over six years—but they often come without the level of grassroots involvement needed to ensure that money targets the real, on-the-ground priorities.

The ambition of the federal government to lock in city prices for essential goods in remote locations seemed promising on the surface, yet the policy design remained predominantly directed by bureaucrats and political leaders who may never have stepped foot into these communities or engaged deeply with local perspectives. Similarly, educational and nutritional initiatives, along with early interventions for domestic violence, appeared on government agendas repeatedly, but they were rarely coupled with sustained, community-driven planning and follow-up. Consequently, any temporary gains risked collapsing once the initial funding period ended, when political attention drifted elsewhere, or if there was a change of government which, essentially, is a possibility at every federal election.

What frustrates many Indigenous advocates is the predictable cycle in which governments promise solutions, impose them, and then wonder why they failed to deliver real change. Initiatives that claimed to promote economic development or employment opportunities tended to be designed with minimal input from those who experienced them firsthand.

As a result, the root causes of entrenched disadvantage—such as generational trauma, land dispossession, and the erosion of cultural identity—are left untouched. Another consequence of this misguided approach is the empowerment of voices that sowed division. When there was little clarity about how and why investments were made, or when community consultation was superficial, critics stepped in and questioned the very rationale for supporting Indigenous programs at all. People who harboured prejudices or self-interest—the ones who were so prominent during the Voice to Parliament campaign in 2023—found it easy to fill the vacuum with misleading claims about wasted funds or preferential treatment. Their message then gained traction in the absence of decisive, transparent strategies that could have been formulated from the ground up.

Rather than focusing on the structural issues that continued to replicate disadvantage, the spotlight always fell on whether funding was justified or whether diverse communities truly needed additional support. The result was a deepening gulf that became more apparent, ensuring that the top-down script—where government agencies usually devised solutions in isolation—remained unchallenged. If this pattern is not broken, the likelihood is high that in another five or six years, a new set of *Closing the Gap* statistics will emerge with the same results, and the cycle of well-meaning but ultimately ineffective policies will just keep rolling on.

THE POLITICAL REALITY: INDIGENOUS ISSUES AS A LOW PRIORITY

This *Closing the Gap* report, the second one to appear after the failure of the 2023 Voice to Parliament referendum, confirmed an obvious political truth: there were few electoral rewards in pushing forward with Indigenous issues, and that reality dampened the likelihood of any bold policy changes.

While a successful referendum in 2023 would not have solved the perennial problems outlined in the report in an instant, the Voice was at least intended to lay foundational structures and bolster long-term efforts in Reconciliation. Instead, its defeat served as a clear signal that politicians could rally more votes by opposing Indigenous measures than by advocating for them, and it emboldened those who viewed any expression of Indigenous recognition—be it dual place names or acknowledgment of Country—as unnecessary or even offensive.

There were flow-on effects from this: some sporting bodies such as the National Rugby League, once keen to display cultural inclusivity, stepped back from practices such as Welcome to Country ceremonies to commence a game; politicians such as Peter Dutton gleefully refused to stand in front of Indigenous flags during media conferences; and public criticism of everyday gestures of respect became more pronounced.

As these symbolic gestures were gradually removed, the deeper structural challenges remained unaddressed. Critics argue that Welcome to Country ceremonies didn't address any of these structural challenges, so they should be removed, yet fail to put forward the evidence that removing them would improve these challenges. How many suicides were prevented by Dutton's refusal to stand before an Indigenous flag?

The Country Liberal government in the Northern Territory cancelled its Treaty process, and the new Liberal–National Party government in Queensland followed suit, and this was part of a broader conservative retreat from meaningful actions to recognise Indigenous people. The political calculation had been made—as well as an ideological commitment—that there was little benefit in promoting these initiatives, especially when vocal conservative segments of the electorate, resentful of being reminded of contested histories that might somehow disadvantage them, actively push back against acknowledgments of dispossession and calls for justice.

None of this was surprising, especially in a nation that had long been uneasy with confronting the implications of the Mabo decision from 1992 and the idea of living on stolen land. This entrenched discomfort reflects a refusal to deal with historic truths and their modern-day consequences. Yet the aftermath of the Voice referendum and the accompanying backlash to Indigenous recognition were not solely about stagnation; they also represented a culture war flashpoint where opposing progress was framed as defending tradition.

Those who questioned or critiqued entrenched racism usually ignited a defensive response, the *I'm not racist, but* response that denied the underlying prejudice. At the same time, societal standards of what was deemed overtly racist evolved over several generations to be more critical of harmful language and attitudes. This slow but perceptible shift, though positive in some respects, remains woefully insufficient in addressing the multilayered disadvantage captured by the *Closing the Gap* figures.

It is this disconnect—where greater public sensitivity to explicit racism coexists with a reluctance to reform entire systems—that the persistent inequities endured. Despite repeated evidence of widespread suffering and missed opportunities for Indigenous communities, the release of the *Closing the Gap* report barely registered in political headlines.

Prime Minister Anthony Albanese delivered the *Closing the Gap* report during the week, almost as a perfunctory duty, and then quickly moved to other matters: again, emphasising the perception that there was no substantial electoral reward in advocating for Indigenous affairs, as Albanese discovered during the Voice to Parliament referendum. Beyond the corridors of power, however, there remained a hope that this annual reminder of widening gaps would eventually prompt more people to press for action. The dream is that one day, enough policymakers and members of the public will begin to see Indigenous wellbeing not as a niché cause or a tokenistic gesture, but as a matter of national responsibility, moral necessity, and, ultimately, collective benefit. Until then, the cycle of disappointing statistics and half-hearted proposals continue, overshadowed by the reality that, for now, political capital still lay elsewhere, especially in the lead-up to the federal election campaign.

MANUFACTURING OUTRAGE WITH ZIONIST PROVOCATEURS

An incident in late February in Sydney's Inner West raised many questions about the manipulation and creation of anti-Semitic incidents in Australia by right-wing extremists and agitators in the lead-up to the federal election. Ofir Birenbaum, a prominent member of the controversial Australian Jewish Association and a known Zionist provocateur, attempted to manufacture an incident at the Cairo Takeaway cafe in Newtown where, wearing a Star of David cap, he tried to provoke a hostile or anti-Semitic reaction that could be captured by *Daily Telegraph* reporters waiting outside.

The goal was to create a sensational story about rampant anti-Semitism in Australia, push a narrative of an under-protected Jewish community and, in turn, continue to launch political attacks against the Labor government in the lead-up to the election campaign. Yet in Newtown—a suburb well-known for its diversity and inclusive culture—the provocation didn't succeed: Birenbaum's actions were met with disinterest, and a *best to leave this dickhead alone* approach. No matter what he tried, staff and patrons at the cafe simply went about their day. Consequently, not only did the *Daily Telegraph* fail to get the inflammatory story they were after, it also exposed the larger dynamics between right-wing media outlets and extremist pro-Israel activists who collaborate to manipulate public sentiment.

The issue goes beyond this one incident: Rupert Murdoch's media empire has a long record of backing pro-Israel positions and narratives, with coverage that is often supportive of the Israel's government and policies, leaving no room for more nuanced or critical perspectives. Such one-sided messaging deepens community tensions, stirs up Islamophobia, and delegitimises anyone critical of Israel's policies by painting them as prejudiced or anti-Semitic.

In many cases, it works because they exploit the fear of anti-Semitism—which, of course, is a very real phenomenon—and exaggerate or manufacture incidents to heighten public anxiety. This approach not only fuels prejudice toward other communities, particularly Muslim and Middle Eastern Australians, but it also distracts from legitimate discussions about the Israeli government's controversial policies, such as settlement expansion in the West Bank, the unresolved status of the occupied territories, or the attempts of genocide in Gaza.

Birenbaum's failed attempt to manufacture outrage revealed how much of a miscalculation it can be to try such a stunt in an area like Newtown, where cultural diversity is part of everyday life. Here, anyone is generally free to dress and express themselves as they please, religious symbols included. Ironically, his actions inadvertently shone a light on exactly how certain factions are trying to foment hatred, and strengthened the resolve to reject such divisive tactics in the process.

Beyond this incident, there was a concern about a wider pattern of racially motivated violence and intimidation. Recent incidents, such as two women being assaulted in Epping in Melbourne—one of them pregnant and choked with her own hijab—remind us that hate crimes and racism of all types must be taken seriously. The police response to these cases was relatively slow, which raises other questions about biases in law enforcement.

What emerged from all of this was how particular media operators and ideologically driven individuals can collude to manufacture controversies for political advantage. Broader debates about Israel—whether it pertains to its establishment, the 1948 or 1967 borders, the ongoing violent settlement and policies, or genocide in Gaza—need to occur in an environment where all voices can be heard, without fear of being automatically labeled as hostile to an entire group of people.

ONE-SIDED POLITICAL RESPONSES HAVE AIDED THE OUTRAGE

Australia's political leaders often position themselves as staunch opponents of racial or religious hatred, yet their actions frequently reveal a very different story. In the aftermath of this failed provocation in Newtown, the conspicuous silence from key figures, including the Prime Minister, Anthony Albanese, showed how officials can shrink from manipulative media narratives—especially when they originate from powerful outlets.

The fact that this incident took place in Albanese's own electorate of Grayndler without so much as a public statement of support for the workers at the Cairo Takeaway cafe spoke volumes. Political leaders are busy people, but they often find the time to comment on a range of local matters, and it would not have been unreasonable for the Prime Minister or even the New South Wales Premier, Chris Minns, to express concern or, at the very least, check on the concerns of a business drawn into a media stunt. That nothing of the sort happened fuels the double standard, where criticism or scrutiny of certain individuals or groups is all but off-limits and the political class mostly looks away.

It seemed that nobody in government wanted to risk the wrath of a media apparatus that holds the power to amplify or dampen political fortunes. As a result, the government's message to the public is one of tacit acceptance, suggesting that if powerful media barons or well-connected interest groups orchestrate disinformation, officials will quietly stand aside.

The weakness of political leadership is also apparent when sensational, potentially harmful media stories go unchallenged. An example of this was the *Sydney Morning Herald*'s report about a caravan allegedly loaded with explosives on the outskirts of Sydney and a supposed list of Jewish targets. Their alarmist headlines—which were then magnified in other media outlets— implied Australia was on the verge of a serious terrorist plot, but the follow-up revealed that the explosives were decades old, likely to be inactive, and that the "list" of targets just didn't exist.

Despite the story's debunking, there was no *mea culpa* from either the newspaper or public officials who might have questioned the narrative's origins. Instead, the correction was buried, and the fleeting panic it caused lingered in the public consciousness. Such episodes show how easy it is for the media to manufacture panic that benefits specific agendas, with little pushback from political leaders who ought to defend the public's right to fair and accurate information.

By tolerating these fabrications, or at least failing to challenge them, political leaders enabled a climate of mounting tension. When false or exaggerated stories about anti-Semitic plots are circulated, it leads to inflated fears within Jewish communities. Meanwhile, some in the broader public grow cynical, feeling that accusations of bigotry and hatred are wielded more like political tools than genuine concerns—which then dilutes the seriousness of real incidents of anti-Semitism.

This same dynamic spills over into other forms of prejudice, including Islamophobia, contributing to an atmosphere where the term "hate crime" can be weaponised for political point-scoring rather than addressing actual offenses. Ultimately, those who face genuine discrimination, whether they be Jewish, Muslim, or any other group—are left in a precarious position, unprotected by political leaders who are more interested in appeasement rather than principled leadership.

The real tragedy here is that such timid political responses harm both majority and minority communities. They allow extremist viewpoints—those that genuinely do advocate racist or hateful ideologies, such as News Corporation—to flourish amid the loud noises of manufactured outrage. By not calling out hoaxes out with the same force used against legitimate cases of discrimination, the government placed all of these incidents on the same level, fostering public confusion and weakening the seriousness of legitimate concerns. This environment emboldened individuals who truly harbor anti-Semitic or

Islamophobic sentiments, giving them more credibility than they should ever have. It also undermined the possibility of critical debate about foreign and domestic policy related to Israel, Palestine, and other contentious issues.

What was needed was simple yet it remained elusive: principled leadership willing to hold media organisations accountable, regardless of the political risk, combined with a commitment to confronting bigotry in all its forms. When politicians refuse to waver in the face of powerful media proprietors, they send a clear message that weaponising hatred for clicks, sales, or political favour will not be tolerated. Conversely, by not doing anything about these issues, it suggests that these political leaders either condone the behaviour, or are simply too weak and lack the courage to call out these manipulations, regardless of the source.

THE SILENT STRINGS: HOW THE ISRAEL LOBBY MUTES CRITICISM

One of the other parts of the ongoing manipulation in Australia's public debate is the growing list of individuals who find their voices muzzled the moment they challenge or question Israel's policies. From the journalist Antoinette Lattouf to the academic Tim Anderson, or the artist Khaled Sabsabi, whose commission at the 2026 Venice Biennale was withdrawn by Creative Australia, each example shows a pattern of swift and disproportionate retaliation. Instead of open dialogue or genuine engagement with the substance of their critiques, these people have faced professional setbacks, terminations, and erasure from cultural and academic institutions.

The rationale is almost always vague—somehow "offensive" work or "controversial" statements—while the real story, as many suspect, is that a small, well-connected lobby exerted influence behind the scenes, by threats of withdrawing funding or other retaliations. When art containing images of the Palestinian flag is quietly censored—the National Art Gallery in Canberra censored the tapestry created by the art collective SaVĀge K'lub—or individuals are dropped from high-profile exhibitions without transparent explanations, it's obvious that the criticism of Israel is being relegated to the margins in a supposedly free society.

What makes this trend unacceptable is that it dismantles the very principles that Australian democracy claims to hold dear. The nature of academic inquiry is supposed to be rigorous, involving a contest of ideas tested against facts and peer review. If a professor calls Israel an apartheid state—as Tim Anderson did in 2018—a proper response should emerge through research and debate rather than abrupt dismissal.

The same principle applies to the arts; creative expression often provokes discomfort or controversy, and that is precisely its job. By punishing artists who reflect on real-world conflicts, cultural institutions abandon their commitment to diverse perspectives. In these acts of censorship or "quiet removals," officials are placating a tiny but influential lobby, stifling conversation on issues that deeply affect Australia's multicultural population. Meanwhile, the broader public is left wondering why certain topics are off-limits and who decides that some viewpoints must vanish without explanation.

This climate is evolving into a modern-day McCarthyism, in which the smallest suspicion of being "too critical" of Israel triggers punitive measures. For those who stand up for Palestinians, it can feel like a precarious balancing act. Rather than fostering a safe environment for legitimate dissent, Australia's institutions are sending a message: *speak out and you will be removed.* The result inhibits not only controversial or provocative voices but also anyone who might support them. Eventually, public debate becomes sterile, absent of the kind of fearless, critical thought that marks a robust and healthy democracy. And this, ultimately, is not good for *any* democracy.

Yet this level of censorship, even if it might be effective in the short term, rarely silences an idea *forever*. The anger it generates often leads to stronger, more unified calls for change. As more people notice the removal of dissenting voices, they begin to question the motives and the power structures behind such decisions. Although censorship in Australia on behalf of the state of Israel may not be on the scale of the United States, where media consolidation and lobbying are furiously ridiculous, bordering on fascism, the echoes in Australia are loud enough to raise alarm.

It's unlikely to happen, but this is the moment that demands courage from those who occupy positions of influence, whether in government, media, academia, or the arts. People who promote free speech and the right to critique power must be willing to protect those who offer inconvenient truths or unpopular perspectives. The irony is that open debate would likely strengthen Australia's institutions; it would give communities—Jewish, Muslim, or otherwise—more confidence that concerns and criticisms can be aired without fear of reprisal and the refusal to engage openly simply breeds more mistrust.

No matter how strong the attempt to silence critics, the fundamental issues remain: the complex reality of the Israel–Palestine conflict, the consequences of foreign policy decisions, and the moral questions raised by longstanding military occupations, genocide and human rights abuses. Suppressing discussion about these matters only heightens divisions, disenfranchises the marginalised, and allows genuine extremism to grow in the shadows, such as the extremism that is promoted by News Corporation.

Australia's best defence against imported hatred and internal strife is a forthright commitment to democratic values—ones that do not kotow to pressure from any lobby, no matter how well-funded or influential. It doesn't require additional protection, just application of the laws *as they exist*: protecting those who challenge entrenched power structures, insisting on transparency in decision-making, and standing up for the free flow of ideas—even when doing this poses a risk. Only then can a functional, pluralistic Australia thrive, unburdened by the question of whose voices are being silenced, and why.

AUSTRALIA'S POLL FRENZY AND UNBELIEVABLE PRO-DUTTON SPIN

The release of a batch of opinion polls in late February unleashed a fury of media attention, with the narrative forced down our throats that the Liberal and National Coalition were set to win the federal election. The YouGov/MRP poll—the one that got all the attention—delivered its headline forecasting a Coalition win and the supposed crowning of Dutton as the 32nd prime minister, who'd soon be residing in The Lodge. The basis for these claims remained tenuous—aside from the small matter of an election that had to be held before these claims could be realised, and it was the electorate that made the decision, not the opinion pollsters—nevertheless, the mainstream media seized upon the poll's figures with their usual enthusiasm, pushing the idea that a new era of conservative leadership was imminent, with a big hooray!

This was taken to fever pitch by other outlets such as the ABC, which hyped the possibility of a Dutton-led government and eagerly speculated on what Coalition policies might mean for everyday Australians. While the public coverage was breathless, one couldn't ignore the gleeful tone of certain commentators who seemed more than happy to help paint the Coalition's path to victory as a *fait accompli*, one that would surely be rubber-stamped by the electorate at the election.

However, beneath the headlines—the ones that verged on propaganda or were *actual* propaganda—a more cautious view suggested that these polling numbers were far from conclusive. The YouGov/MRP data indicated a two-party-preferred figure of 49 per cent for Labor and 51 per cent for the Coalition, with the claim that the Coalition was well-positioned to form a minority government. Poll-driven coverage often benefits the pollsters themselves, who receive substantial publicity and reinforce their own brands each time a "shock" result or dramatic insight captivates the media.

It also met the mainstream media's hunger for compelling narratives that kept audiences engaged and promoted a conservative agenda. Casting Labor in a precarious position suited the interests of media outlets that thrived on the spectacle of tight electoral contests—and once again, it was the spectacle of what the academic Jay Rosen referred to as 'horse-race journalism'. While it always remains possible that the prediction of an opinion might prove accurate, it's essential to note that highly speculative figures do not translate to guaranteed outcomes, and in the case of the final election on May 3, they were proven to be totally incorrect. The real test always takes place on election day, and these sorts of data points—published months out from the election—risk becoming self-fulfilling prophecies only if they generated so much noise that they started to influence voter perception and behaviour.

Further complicating the picture was the divergence of results across other pollsters. Resolve, through Nine Media, reported a far wider gap, with a 55–45 per cent split favouring the Coalition, as if to say to YouGov/MRP: "*that's* not a headline, *this* is a headline". This finding was splashed across newspapers and online forums, seemingly confirming the idea that Labor's position was on shaky ground and they were definitely on track to lose the federal election.

But an almost concurrent Morgan poll that had Labor at 51.5 per cent and the Coalition at 48.5 per cent almost received no media attention at all. This selective reporting—in which polls featuring dramatic, headline-grabbing numbers received more coverage—highlighted the tendency for the media to elevate stories that fed sensational narratives, while more moderate or contradictory data was minimised or just ignored. The result was a skewed picture for the public, with each polling result touted or downplayed depending on how well it supported the storyline that a new Coalition government under Dutton was on the horizon. And, to use the words of former prime minister Paul Keating, who described Dutton as the "most wicked and cynical of individuals," if that were to happen, *God help us*.

Amid all the noise, the practical question of how any incoming prime minister would form government remained unanswered. Manufactured rumours swirled about which independents or smaller parties might be willing to line up with the Liberal and National Coalition if a hung parliament eventuated. The community independents, who had largely parted ways with the Liberal Party over policy differences that reflected "Duttonesque" hardline stances, were not an obvious fit for a Coalition agreement. Why would they?

Similarly, Bob Katter might not have been guaranteed to align with the Coalition simply because of his usual conservative leanings. Political negotiations involving independents rarely occurred in a vacuum of *left vs. right* calculations, as we saw in 2010, when the right-leaning independents Tony Windsor and Rob Oakeshott guaranteed a minority government for Julia Gillard, rather than side with the conservative Tony Abbott; personal relationships, local concerns, and policy priorities all factored into how votes on the floor of parliament aligned.

The increasingly dire opinion polling picture for Labor, at least as presented by the sensational media coverage, had overshadowed these nitty-gritty details of potential post-election horse trading. Nonetheless, these details mattered, since they would shape whether a minority government could even be formed by the Coalition, let alone governed effectively over a full term. In the end, the real power remained with Australian voters, who tended to be cautious about delivering sweeping changes unless there was a strong impetus to do so. Historical voting patterns suggested that electorates did not usually shift dramatically unless confronted by significant dissatisfaction or compelling alternatives.

For all the talk of a "predestined" future prime minister in Dutton, the evidence for such a prediction in the polls was not as rock solid as the media frenzy suggested. It's a cliché but *the only poll that mattered was on election day*, and while some journalists and commentators continued to promote the sensational possibilities highlighted by YouGov/MRP and others, a more measured analysis called for a significant level of skepticism.

It was entirely possible that a minority Labor government could still emerge from these same numbers, once the independent seats and coalition-building realities came into play. Even if the polling remained shaky in the lead-up, election outcomes depend on a mixed web of preferences, regional fluctuations, last-minute swings, and the elusive mood of the electorate, none of which could ever be perfectly captured by a single poll or even a series of them.

AN UNCHARTED POLITICAL TERRAIN: WHY PREDICTIONS FELL FLAT AT THE ELECTION

In the lead-up to an election already defined by headline-grabbing polls and breathless media coverage, the biggest revelation had been how deeply the uncertainty had set in. While most of the commentary had concentrated on the shortcomings of both Anthony Albanese and Dutton as prime ministers, there was a more seismic factor looming: according to these opinion polls, an estimated 42 per cent of the electorate planned to vote for minor parties or independents. While it ended up being around 35 per cent by the time of the election, this shift brought an unpredictable measure that neither major party could confidently navigate, no matter how many polls or pundits predicted otherwise—what we witnessed was the accelerated erosion of the two-party system's dominance.

With such a large proportion of votes falling outside the traditional Coalition-versus-Labor binary, the critical issue at the election was how preferences flowed and how effectively each party adjusted to this splintered environment. Governments usually rely on incumbency to have the polling numbers drift back to them as the election day draws closer. However, the conventional notion that elections were decided on the single day at the ballot box had quickly become outdated—in recent elections, including in 2025, almost half of the electorate voted in the two or three weeks of the prepoll period, and this factor forced campaigns to sustain their messaging and momentum over a longer period of time. Parties that treated those final fourteen days as just a prelude to election day risked forfeiting a large level of potential support to opponents or to the minor parties and community-backed independents who had become increasingly adept at targeting local concerns.

This more fluid environment also aligned with ongoing generational and philosophical evolutions in Australian politics. Voters were no longer content to accept party machines designed in the industrial ages, when labour and capital were the core political battlegrounds. The rise of concerns such as climate change, technological disruption, and cultural diversity had strained these old frameworks. When 35 per cent of people gravitate to minor parties or independents, it's because they are not finding answers in the traditional spectrum of left versus right within the major parties, but are instead searching for candidates and platforms that aligned more closely with specific policy priorities or localised viewpoints.

In this context, the big parties found many of their long-held beliefs or strategies rendered not necessarily wrong, but irrelevant. Consequently, it was entirely possible that every bit of conventional wisdom regarding party swings, incumbency benefits, and leadership drags broke down in the face of a fast-changing political landscape, leaving pundits and pollsters scrambling to explain an outcome few had foreseen.

CAUTION BECAME A LIABILITY: LABOR'S TIMIDITY GAVE DUTTON A PLATFORM

It remained seriously bewildering that a Labor government found itself languishing in the polls against Dutton—even though these were just opinion polls and were proven to be incorrect—many considered Dutton to be among the least capable opposition leaders in recent Australian political history and totally unfit to be the prime minister. There were many factors here: Albanese's attempt to lower the political temperature, as he said soon after becoming prime minister—a move initially welcomed by a public weary of relentless combativeness.

Yet, by pulling back so far, Labor surrendered the narrative to the Coalition, allowing it to frame debates and fill the media vacuum with noise and political theatre. This style of "quiet" leadership might have soothed the electorate in less tumultuous times, but in a climate where opinion polls already struggled to account for the massive 35 per cent supporting minor parties and independents, a lack of boldness gave the Coalition room to seize the agenda.

Labor's core dilemma was that it was no longer enough simply to coast on incumbency. There is a nostalgia for leaders such as Whitlam, Hawke, Keating, and even Rudd or Gillard, and all of them carried grand ambitions when they were in office. By comparison, Albanese's incremental approach, designed to avoid the pitfalls of polarising conflict, did little to energise the base or capture the enthusiasm of the public.

Even if there were strong arguments for a more measured style of governance—particularly in an era keen to reject the hyper-partisanship that had permeated politics globally—those arguments lost weight when a government slipped behind in the polls to a party thought by many to be in internal disarray. Add to this the sobering memories of 2019, when Bill Shorten was widely expected to become prime minister right up until the point that he didn't, and Labor's margin for error narrowed further. Polls can be fickle and sometimes failed to detect shifts in public sentiment until it was too late, yet they still set narratives that influence whether a political party was viewed as confident or vulnerable.

The historical parallel with John Hewson's failed bid in 1993 highlighted how a supposedly lacklustre government could still outsmart an opposition leader plagued by overconfidence. Just as Hewson was undone by a combination of unpopular policies and campaign missteps despite vocal media backing, there were clear pathways for Dutton to stumble spectacularly. His popularity numbers, while occasionally buoyed by headlines predicting a miracle Coalition comeback, still fell short of the massive advantage required to snatch a substantial number of seats from Labor in a single election. A wide gulf separated media hype from concrete electoral gains—yet each day that passed without a clear, stirring vision from Labor made it more feasible for the Coalition to cobble together enough momentum to threaten a return to government.

The final challenge for Labor was that its timid approach unfolded in an era of rapid political transformation. If Labor persisted with a defensive strategy, it risked further losing support to newcomers in the electorate—the community independents—and to the Australian Greens or other minor parties. No amount of incumbency advantage could fully withstand a rising tide of disillusionment when policy ambition appeared lukewarm.

In a contest described as one of the most unpredictable in decades, the feeling was that it was possible the government would prevail once voters took a closer look at Dutton in a full campaign spotlight—he had avoided scrutiny for most of that parliamentary term but during an election campaign, there was nowhere to hide. However, without a clear sense of bold purpose, Labor inadvertently risked transforming an ordinary and mediocre opponent into a genuine threat. In a political environment *that* volatile, caution became a liability faster than any poll could predict—and if Labor wished to hold on to power, it needed the same force of vision that once defined the party's greatest leaders.

THE CRACKS IN THE EMPIRE: AMERICA'S ALLIES DRIFT AWAY

By March, most of the Western world had been preparing for a shift in their relationship with the United States, as the once-unshakable alliances that defined global politics in the post-war and Cold War eras began to erode, replaced by a cautious pragmatism among America's closest partners. The assumption that Washington would always be the uncontested leader of the free world was being reconsidered as allies—quietly or openly—recalibrated their strategic positions.

The dynamic between the United States and its allies changed dramatically, and trade disputes, inconsistent foreign policies, domestic upheaval, and an erratic approach to international commitments led these partners to reassess their long-standing ties. Canada responded with its own economic measures, imposing tariffs in retaliation.

Its then-Prime Minister Justin Trudeau went beyond traditional diplomatic protests, urging Canadians to personally disengage from American economic and cultural products, when he suggested "we're going to choose not to go on vacation in Florida... we're going to choose to try to buy Canadian products and forego American products... and, we're probably going to keep booing the American anthem". These remarks were made not from a fringe activist but from the leader of a G7 nation—a clear sign that even America's closest neighbours has grown weary of Washington's shifting priorities.

The British government firmed up its stance on NATO, evidence of its frustration with the American leadership, and in the post-Brexit landscape, increasingly sought to redefine its role within the Western alliance.

Yet, despite these global undercurrents, Australia remained notably silent. Unlike Canada and Britain, where leaders at least acknowledged changing realities, both the Australian government and the opposition continued to echo the same unwavering rhetoric about the U.S. alliance. The usual platitudes regarding American leadership were repeated with near-religious fervour, while the rest of the world watched and wondered—why are they doing that?

For decades, Australia had been a steadfast ally of the United States, but history has shown that this loyalty has not always been reciprocated. Australia followed the U.S. into Vietnam under questionable circumstances, joined wars in Iraq—twice, despite widespread skepticism—and committed forces to Afghanistan, a conflict that, in hindsight, offered little strategic benefit to Canberra or, perhaps, even to the United States.

Yet, Canberra's alignment with American interests remained like an instinctive reflex action, as if questioning the alliance is taboo and diplomatically unpalatable. This loyalty contrasted with the aggressive approaches of other Western allies, who reasserted their independence on global security and economic policy.

Despite these realities, the shifting nature of the U.S.–Australia relationship was downplayed at home. This alliance should have been a major political issue in the lead-up to the election—a topic of national debate and even an election-defining discussion—but it wasn't. Instead, it remained cloaked in an aura of unbreakable commitment and clichés, ignoring a growing sense that Washington was no longer the reliable partner it once was and that this situation had changed rapidly.

As the world increasingly moved beyond automatic deference to American leadership, Australia was one of the nations still clinging to the old but changing order. But for how much longer? With U.S. influence in flux, the question wasn't whether the alliance would face challenges, but when.

WHY A SUBMISSIVE AUSTRALIA DIDN'T QUESTION THE ALLIANCE

Anthony Albanese's careful approach to foreign policy was nothing new. As a Prime Minister who valued caution and steadiness, he did all he could to keep Australia's alignment with the United States beyond debate. But at what cost? Australia's subservience to Washington has become a self-imposed straightjacket, preventing any meaningful discussion of what the nation actually gained from this long-standing arrangement.

Peter Dutton, meanwhile, never contemplated opposing U.S. policy, as his instincts and behaviours mirrored hardline Trumpian Republican stances. The Coalition opposition, much like Labor, seemed intent on avoiding any debate over U.S.–

Australia relations, preferring to stick to the grandiose talking points about the "unbreakable" bond between the two nations. Yet this tactic became less tenable. The geopolitical landscapes evolve, and sooner or later, Australia will have to confront an uncomfortable question: beyond serving American strategic interests, what exactly does this alliance achieve for Australia?

Australia's role as Washington's obedient partner is well documented. Pine Gap? Created in 1966 without hesitation, and even led indirectly to the dismissal of prime minister Gough Whitlam, after he had considered closing the base down in 1975 after the completion of the initial nine-year treaty. Troops to Iraq and Afghanistan? No resistance and presented without debate. AUKUS? A staggering $368 billion for nuclear submarines that may never be delivered. The pattern is clear: the U.S. demands, and Australia complies. This is not a partnership in the true sense—it's deference, with Canberra appearing more eager to placate Washington than assert its own national interests.

Despite this track record, foreign policy is largely absent from Australia's political conversations. It's rarely discussed during election campaigns, partly because neither major party can see any benefit in doing so, and the last time foreign affairs took centre stage in an Australian election was in 2001, under the shadow of the 9/11 attacks in New York. Since then, talk of Australia's global position has been side-lined, and political leaders prioritised domestic concerns which, of course, is understandable—domestic concerns will always trump international issues when it comes to elections in Australia. But that silence can't last forever.

The United States was growing more unpredictable by the day, yet Australia remained unwilling to acknowledge it. While Canada adopted retaliatory economic measures and Britain quietly distanced itself from certain American military positions, Australia clung to habit. Even the Labor Party, historically more inclined to question blind loyalty to Washington, avoided breaking ranks, perhaps in the fear that the Coalition could exploit any deviation on national security grounds.

Still, Australia is not without leverage. Though it may lack Canada's economic might or Britain's global weight, it still has options—particularly concerning AUKUS. This was hastily brokered under the unpopular Morrison government in 2021, and even Donald Trump seemed to be unaware of agreement when asked about it.

If a future U.S. administration deprioritised or cancelled it, Australia would have little to show for a massive financial outlay. Even Elbridge Colby, Trump's nominee for undersecretary of defense, suggested selling submarines to Australia under AUKUS would be "crazy" if tensions between China and Taiwan arose. Renegotiating—or withdrawing altogether from the AUKUS deal—would not have been an act of rebellion but a rational move in the country's own interest.

The British Prime Minister, Keir Starmer, has already shown that challenging U.S. policy need not destroy alliances. His public support for Ukraine, despite America's antagonism towards President Volodymyr Zelenskyy, proved that a nation could maintain strong ties with Washington while exercising its own judgment, and Australia had every right to do likewise. The concern that any challenge to U.S. policy might lead to political backlash ignored the reality that many voters were ambivalent or would have actually favoured a reassessment: according to the Pew Research Center, 60 per cent of Australians in 2024 had an unfavourable view of the United States, a number which would have dropped even further since the inauguration of Trump in early 2025.

The real question was whether anyone in Canberra had the courage to act. Maintaining the status quo—quietly accepting every American directive while pretending there was nothing to discuss—may have seemed like the easiest option, but it was just an illusion. As global circumstances change, this silence will break—whether through political upheaval, electoral realignment, or pure necessity. The only uncertainty was whether Australia would set its own course or simply react when it could no longer avoid doing so.

AUSTRALIA MUST STAND UP AND RECLAIM ITS NATIONAL INTEREST

For too long, Australia has walked on eggshells with its relationship with the United States, as though any minor step away from a complete alignment would be catastrophic. But standing up to Washington need not have been reckless; instead, it would have affirmed Australia's sovereignty. Far from weakening the alliance, it could bolster it by establishing a more balanced and transparent foundation. Politically, challenging the U.S. might even prove to be advantageous.

Given this situation, what was the Albanese government so afraid of? The U.S. is a powerful country but it's not invincible. Its leadership is becoming more chaotic, and its strategic goals have shifted unpredictably. Blindly adhering to Washington—

despite self-destructive or counterproductive policies—was not sound diplomacy; it was submission, and no self-respecting country should have placed itself in this position.

Honesty was what the alliance lacked the most. Simon Crean, the then opposition leader in 2003, made that clear when he told U.S. President George W. Bush that true friends can disagree, emphasising that "honesty is the foundation stone of that great Australian value, mateship". That kind of candour has been missing from Australia's foreign policy for years.

No one expected Albanese to confront the United States aggressively, even if he should have. No one suggested he threaten to close Pine Gap in protest over tariffs or military policy which, as Whitlam discovered in 1975, could have been a politically dangerous move for him. But acknowledging that the alliance was deeply skewed would have been a start. Whether it's AUKUS, the Iraq War, Afghanistan, or trade disputes, Australia often bends to American demands in exchange for little more than vague assurances of security and partnership.

This lack of transparency extends beyond defence matters to the broader political landscape. Politicians, the media, and the political establishment rarely address the reality that the U.S. often treats Australia as a subordinate. When Western Australian Premier Roger Cook candidly called U.S. Vice-President J.D. Vance a "knob" and suggested that Trump represented uncertainty—if not outright danger—he gave voice to what many people already believed. The fact that this moment of honesty was so surprising illustrated the deep-seated reluctance to discuss Australia's true status in this alliance.

THE CRACKS IN THE EMPIRE: AMERICA'S ALLIES DRIFT AWAY

If a state premier could speak frankly, why couldn't the Prime Minister? Why couldn't federal leaders question American policies that didn't align with Australian interests? Why must major defence and foreign policy decisions be rubber-stamped by Washington before Canberra can even debate them?

Australia's alleged lack of leverage is often cited as an excuse for inaction, but that rationale doesn't hold water. Britain showed that even the closest U.S. allies could stand firm when they chose. Canada levied tariffs in defiance of American economic pressure. Smaller nations across Europe and the Pacific asserted their independence when dealing with Washington.

There were many things Australia could have done. It could have rethought its participation in American military ventures and avoided being dragged into conflicts irrelevant to its own security. It could have used its influence in the Pacific and southeast Asia to balance China on Australia's terms, rather than uncritically following U.S. directives, which ultimately damaged Australia's diplomatic, economic and political interests.

Stepping away from automatic deference is not disloyalty; it's an act of self-respect. It would have signalled to Washington that Australia is an equal partner, not a subservient ally. Crucially, it could also have been politically advantageous—the Australian electorate was far from oblivious to the dysfunction in Washington.

Before long, the U.S. alliance inevitably will become a national issue, as global events changed too rapidly for America's dominance to continue unchecked. The real question is whether Australia can redefine its global role proactively or wait until circumstances forced it to respond. If it waited, it risked missing a critical chance to reshape its position on its own terms. If it acted, Australia may finally have gained a more balanced and honest partnership with the United States—one that primarily serves Australian interests.

A BETTER ECONOMY BUT DID LABOR SELL THE GOOD NEWS?

The Australian economy was showing signs of a meaningful recovery in March, shifting away from a per capita recession—for nearly seven years, covering most of the final years of the Morrison government and the first two and a half years of the Albanese government, there wasn't much room for economic optimism. Yet, the trajectory at the time suggested a marked improvement, backed by several important indicators: inflation fell dramatically, interest rates eased (slightly), employment strengthened, and incomes gradually rose.

Federal Treasurer Jim Chalmers promoted this situation as a "soft landing," also suggesting that it was an opportunity to stabilise growth without subjecting the community to the harsh elements of an economic recession. Pointing to a range of factors that many nations struggled to achieve simultaneously—reducing inflation, raising wages, lowering unemployment and reducing government debt—but which Australia managed to do, Chalmers highlighted the importance of both public and private sector growth in this equation, which provided some momentum within the Australian economy.

The timing could not have been more critical for a government seeking to leverage good economic news before the election. While the economy was far from reaching peak performance, it certainly improved from the uncertainty of a few years ago, and this upward trend offered a good political backdrop for the Labor government: a government in office generally benefits from positive economic sentiment in the lead-up to an election—not always, but on most occasions—provided it can persuade the public that the gains are genuine and sustainable.

In this respect, the Albanese government seemed well positioned to capitalise on recent data: inflation still needed to come down further for most people to truly feel relief in everyday costs—where prices rarely reverted to cheaper levels but instead rose more slowly—but the gradual easing in cost-of-living pressures added credence to the political message pushed by the government that things were "turning around".

In contrast to past governments that were accused of inflating or misrepresenting Australia's economic figures—the Morrison government was a specialist at this—the narrative in 2025 was supported by the data. Inflation peaked at 7.8 per cent in December 2022, and the figures by early 2025 sat at 2.4 per cent. Interest rates—which commenced increasing after the peak of COVID in 2021, reached 4.35 per cent in November 2023, and eased to 4.1 per cent. The employment-to-population ratio increased to a record high of 64.5 per cent in December 2024, and wages grew 3.5 per cent over the past twelve months according to the wage price index, after going backwards by 3.4 per cent in the five quarters before that.

Consumer prices for everyday essentials still caused anxiety for households, but there were broader signs of structural support, from slight reductions in interest rates to more modest increases in the price of basic goods. This alignment of positive indicators provided the government with an opportunity to craft a strong economic message: lower inflation, manageable interest rates—not great, but manageable—and the potential for wage increases that could create an environment that benefited workers and businesses alike. While Australia was not entirely out of the woods, this improved outlook provided some optimism that resonated well beyond the political class. The electorate, if convinced that better economic circumstances were on the not-too-distant horizon, would reward the government in the election.

That remained the central question though: how effectively could these numbers be communicated so that voters genuinely believed in the changes they were seeing, not just in abstract economic data but in their day-to-day lives? If the economy continued its recovery, the government's ability to merge economic facts with a compelling narrative would set the tone for the election campaign. It really was a matter of whether this government was capable of harnessing the better economic news into a coherent message that appealed to the electorate.

THE COALITION AND MEDIA ALLIES TRIED TO DERAIL LABOR'S ECONOMIC GOOD NEWS

Despite the emerging narrative of Australia's economic improvement, a predictable wave of conservative media coverage centred on discrediting every optimistic data point.

Whenever interest rates dropped or GDP figures rose, conservative media commentators aligned with the Coalition cast doubt, demanding that rates should have been even lower, or that growth needed to be even faster. This cycle repeated itself on nearly every metric: an improvement in employment numbers was dismissed for being not large enough, and news of easing inflation was minimised by comparing it unfavourably to conditions in other countries such as New Zealand or Canada. If the Australian economy ranked second in the International Monetary Fund's world budget management rankings—not good enough, according to the media—why wasn't it number one?

While such criticism could be expected from an opposition party seeking to undermine a government's achievements, the challenge for Labor was that it faced a media environment only too willing to amplify these disparaging media narratives, narratives that are never pushed whenever the Coalition is in office, even when the economic figures are far worse.

When Australia recently exited the per capita recession—a rarely-used and nuanced measure that reflected population numbers relative to economic expansion—this prompted a new twist in the cycle of negativity. Media outlets reluctant to concede any genuine upturn then pointed to government spending or other peripheral factors that ended this per capita recession, unwilling to acknowledge improving fundamentals. Leading the charge was Shadow Treasurer Angus Taylor, who then inexplicably denied that Australia had moved out of a per capita recession—even though the evidence and facts clearly stated that this was the case—with no stronger reason than a desire to sustain his narrative and score political points using falsehoods.

Ultimately, public sentiment hinges on whether people in the electorate experienced better day-to-day conditions. If Australians could be convinced that their household finances were improving and their communities were stabilising, it might have been game over for the Coalition's electoral ambitions, especially given the unpopularity of their leader, Peter Dutton. Certainly, his unpopularity ratings mirrored the unpopularity of the Prime Minister, Anthony Albanese, but it was mirrored in a different way.

Frantic attempts by the media to humanise Dutton—through smiling photo-ops or puff-piece profiles highlighting his personal life—did little to mask questions about his extensive property portfolio, share tradings and a disconnect from the ordinary struggles of the electorate, or his attempts to magnify the issues of terrorism and anti-Semitism.

Voters who found themselves stretched thin by mortgage pressures or rising rents were likely to resent any suggestion that owning more than two dozen properties was just par for the course: it wasn't. Or jetting off to a political fundraiser in Sydney, rather than being with his community in Brisbane during a time of need. Such dissonance made it increasingly difficult for Dutton and his allies in the conservative media to craft a compelling alternative story, one that was capable of overriding the growing perception that the Australian economy, and the daily lives of its citizens, were on the mend.

BIG PROMISES AND POLICY BATTLES

As momentum built toward the federal election, both major parties honed their messages and policy offerings. The Albanese government's strategy centred on social services and education, highlighted by announcements such as major boosts in Medicare funding and a new $5 billion investment to support public schools in New South Wales. In contrast, the Coalition unveiled a $3 billion plan to acquire twenty-eight additional F-35 fighter jets, a move designed to emphasise its national security credentials and feed into a likely scare campaign based around China—even though these jets would have offered no resistance against the Chinese military in the unlikely event of a conflagration and, more importantly, offered little relief to families more concerned about cost of living pressures or health and education for their children.

The Liberal Party lifted heavily from the American conservative playbook, with ideas ranging from reducing the public sector, to ending work-from-home arrangements. Dutton's vow to mandate a full-time office return for public servants, mirroring steps taken by Donald Trump in the United States, already proved to be contentious. Not only did such a policy clash with current workplace flexibility trends—and a federal public service agreement which was in place until 2027—but it also failed to address the broader macroeconomic benefits of hybrid work, ranging from environmental gains to enhanced employee satisfaction and productivity.

This stance was primarily a response from discontented property owners who once enjoyed lucrative rents from shops and offices in central business districts all around the country, yet this response risked alienating everyday Australians who embraced remote and hybrid work. It was a short-sighted attempt to gain favour and support from influential business groups and donors, rather than a policy that met modern social and economic realities.

Faced with a government enjoying an increasingly optimistic economic narrative, the Coalition's scattergun attacks on Labor's initiatives did little to convince an electorate that saw greater value in improved healthcare, better-funded schools, and rising economic indicators than in flashy military contracts. Certainly, the fear and loathing pushed forward by Dutton and the Liberal–National Party resonated with some parts of the electorate but, for a political leader, there had to be a lot more than frightening the community at every opportunity and hoping everything else would just fall into place.

For a public more concerned with whether flexible work arrangements could persist than with whether toothpick-scale jets would fend off a Chinese superpower, the Coalition's campaign planks were out of touch and increasingly negative. In the end, as voters weighed tangible policy wins against ideological posturing, the gulf between promising social investments and recycled talking points from across the Pacific would determine who prevailed at the ballot box.

WOULD DUTTON'S TRUMP-STYLE BLUEPRINT RESONATE WITH THE ELECTORATE?

Dutton clearly aligned himself with the rabid reactionaries within the Republican Party administration in the U.S.—but was this the recipe for electoral success the Liberal Party hoped for? These ideas originated from powerful American billionaires and Chicago-school economics, whose overriding priority was to reduce taxes and strip back public services—more or less implemented by the Liberal Party ever since the Howard government was elected in 1996—initiatives that benefited major corporations but left everyday citizens footing the bill.

If these policies fully took root in Australia, the effect could have been a further shift away from equitable funding mechanisms: imagine adding more regressive taxes like the GST or maintaining out-of-reach education costs through measures akin to America's student debt system, as if Australia's HECS system wasn't bad enough. Neoliberalism has failed across the world and economies sought different solutions in the 2020s and beyond, yet the Liberal Party promised to implement even more neoliberal policies that worked against the interests of the public.

The worry was that Australia, once a global leader in accessible healthcare, affordable higher education, and robust social security and support, risked discarding these achievements for a model that entrenched inequality and fostered a lifetime of indebtedness for those unable to pay. Dutton's enthusiasm for reactionary American-style policy—where everything from healthcare to education was monetised—revealed a lack of originality and a disregard for Australia's own proven successes. While it may have played well with certain segments of the community and the Liberal Party's donor base, the broader electorate questioned whether Trump-era policies, riddled with social divisiveness and economic disparities, were truly suited to Australian conditions.

A BETTER ECONOMY BUT DID LABOR SELL THE GOOD NEWS?

In an environment where the Albanese government highlighted investments in health and education, the Liberal Party's drift toward a Trump-style blueprint raised pressing questions: was this push to replicate Trump's tactics really about governance, or was it simply a matter of political grandstanding that served the few at the expense of the many?

MANUFACTURING FEAR: FAKE TERROR AS A POLITICAL WEAPON

There was a new development in mid-March in the widely-reported terrorist caravan plot and threat from earlier in the year—the threat didn't actually exist. The fabricated nature of this alleged attack—a caravan was found on the outskirts of Sydney supposedly filled with live explosives to be used against synagogues—was clear to those who were willing to scrutinise the incident and ask the right questions. Yet, raising these doubts at the time was met with accusations of anti-Semitism, which provided a convenient deflection from the larger question: who orchestrated the fabrication, and why?

Who knew that the plot was likely a hoax, and when did they know? It seemed that Peter Dutton did know but either deliberately avoided a security briefing in January or denied receiving a briefing, when he actually *did*. The Australian Federal Police were aware at the time that the incident was highly likely to be a hoax but kept this information under wraps to avoid jeopardising their investigation into the origins of the threat—which, on face value, seemed to be a reasonable proposition. But if Dutton was aware early on that the incident was not real, why did he persist in pushing the narrative of a terror threat for political gain?

Throughout February, Dutton continued to exploit this "attack" to fuel anxiety within the Jewish community and amplify a rising tide of antisemitic behaviour. He repeatedly raised his alarmist rhetoric in Parliament and scored political points by constantly framing the government as weak on security, attempting to boost the Liberal Party's 'tough on crime and terror' position while pushing the message that the Albanese government was incompetent in handling national security matters.

Despite the confirmation from the shadow Home Affairs Minister, Senator James Paterson, that the Liberal Party had received a security briefing, Dutton continued to deny any personal knowledge of the hoax at the time. It stretched credibility to believe that the party leader would be left out of such a crucial briefing on national security—and if Dutton truly was uninformed, it then raised questions about why his own party failed to update him. More likely, he was well aware but saw an opportunity for political exploitation.

The complicity in this deception extended beyond federal politics. New South Wales Premier Chris Minns was also privy to the information that this incident was a hoax, yet his government proceeded to fast-track draconian anti-Semitism legislation in response. While combating anti-Semitism is, without question, an issue that needed to be stamped out, Australia already had robust legal frameworks at both state and federal levels to address racism and hate speech. The speed with which these new laws were introduced raised another question:

was it forced by political agendas rather than a genuine concern for Jewish communities?

Even more troubling was the sphere of influence held by extremist Zionist organisations and Israel lobby groups in Australia, who had long pushed for increased criminalisation of criticism against the state of Israel. If this legal path does continue, even journalists and commentators discussing these developments—let alone questioning them or critiquing the issues of concern—could soon be at risk of prosecution. This effect on free speech isn't speculative paranoia; it's a clear direction in which legal frameworks are shifting.

The question of who ultimately benefited from these legislative changes and heightened public fear was critical. If the plot had instead targeted a mosque, a church, a Hindu temple, or any other religious institution, the political response would have been vastly different—we've seen that happen time and again. The selective outrage and opportunistic exploitation of this event reflected a broader strategy: the manipulation of public fear for political and ideological gain.

HOW THE NEW REACTIVE LAWS THREATENED CIVIL LIBERTIES

The consequences of knee-jerk legislation extended far beyond the immediate moment of the political environment in which they were introduced. The New South Wales government's rapid introduction of these new laws not only had troubling implications—they were damaging to the basic principles of democracy, free speech and civil liberties. These laws were passed, even though Minns knew the threat was a fabrication, raising concerns about the motivations behind them and the longer-term ramifications.

Once a government introduced these kinds of security measures, they were never going to be rolled back. Even when such measures are later revealed to have been unnecessary or disproportionate, the act of attempting to repeal them becomes a political minefield. Any future government that attempted to amend or remove these laws would inevitably face accusations of enabling anti-Semitism, even if their only goal was to restore civil liberties that were eroded under false pretences. This was the insidious trap of reactive policymaking: once embedded, these laws become entrenched, unchallengeable, gradually normalised, and weaponised by groups such as the Israel lobby.

The deeper issue was that laws passed in response to hysteria or political pressure were rarely about protecting the public at large. Instead, they served as tools of political leverage for interest groups with a vested stake in controlling public discourse. The new New South Wales laws effectively set a precedent that elevated one particular type of discrimination above all others, making it more difficult to critique specific political movements or international actions—particularly those related to Israel—without the risk of legal repercussions. This was not about addressing genuine hate crimes, which existing laws already covered, but about reshaping the limits of acceptable political discussion.

Once the state grants itself the power to criminalise certain opinions under the broad banner of "anti-Semitism," it's only a matter of time before these laws are used in ways that go far beyond their original intent. Activists who protested against the Israeli government's policies soon found themselves legally silenced, as was the case with the unlawful arrest by U.S. Immigration and Customs Enforcement of permanent resident and Palestinian student activist, Mahmoud Khalil. Academics engaging in legitimate historical analysis were accused of incitement. Journalists who dared to investigate the political influence of foreign lobbies could be prosecuted under the very laws designed to combat extremism. This was the creeping authoritarianism that masqueraded as moral righteousness, and it's precisely how democratic societies slide toward repression under the guise of protection.

The fact that these laws were introduced following a fabricated event made the situation more unacceptable. It also raised the question: if laws could be passed based on an event that never actually happened, what else could be legislated into existence? If politicians and lobby groups could manufacture a crisis, weaponise it for political gain, and then cement their advantage through law, the danger was not just restricted to one particular issue—it was to the entire framework of democratic governance.

AUSTRALIA PLACATED THE ISRAEL LOBBY WHILE NEGLECTING ISLAMIC COMMUNITIES

The political establishment in Australia made its allegiances clear. When it came to support, advocacy, and policy decisions, the Israel lobby enjoyed unwavering, quick, and bipartisan backing, while Palestinian and Islamic communities were usually met with silence, neglect, or outright hostility. From funding allocations to legislative changes, there was a massive imbalance in how these communities were treated, and this situation exposed a deeper political reality: Australia's ruling class was willing to serve the interests of Israel and its allies, even at the expense of its own social cohesion. A Home Affairs report from November 2023 confirmed what many in the Palestinian and Islamic communities had already been feeling for years—there was no place for them in mainstream political discourse. That report warned that the one-sided political support for Israel was creating divisions in Australian society, yet, instead of attempting to bridge these divides, both the government and the opposition doubled down, choosing to amplify their commitment to Israel rather than acknowledge or mitigate the social exclusion of Palestinian and Muslim Australians.

The clearest evidence of this bias was the financial support directed toward different communities. Following the October 7 attacks in 2023 and the subsequent Israeli assault on Gaza, the Australian government provided $7 million to SBS and AAP to "combat misinformation" about Islamic and Palestinian communities. But instead of directing any of that funding to the very communities affected—to organisations on the ground, to Muslim or Palestinian advocacy groups, or to civil society organisations that could have offered direct assistance—every cent went into government-approved media narratives. In contrast, $25 million was provided directly to the Executive Council of Australian Jewry, an organisation that has actively lobbied for pro-Israel policies in Australia. The message from government could not have been clearer: one community was entitled to state-backed advocacy, while the other was deemed a public relations problem to be managed.

This wasn't just about money; it was about the broader institutional landscape. Jewish community groups had the full weight of government support behind them, from new anti-Semitism laws to enhanced security measures—even when the threats they claimed to face turned out to be fabricated. Meanwhile, documented Islamophobic attacks doubled since 2023, and yet there had been no comparable response—no task force, no emergency funding, no high-profile government statements condemning these acts in Parliament.

Why was this happening? The Israel lobby is politically well-organised, well-funded and well-connected to both major political parties, enjoying direct ties to influential figures in media, business and government. And it has the confidence and the swagger to exploit these relationships. In a video exchange in early March, David Adler from the reactionary and aggressive Zionist agitator, Australian Jewish Association, bragged to the Liberal MP, Julian Leeser, that he had compiled a dossier of the "hostile acts by the foreign minister [Penny Wong] and Labor" against Israel and the Jewish community and sent it off to the Israeli Knesset.

In contrast, Palestinian and Muslim advocacy groups had nowhere near the same level of institutional influence and their concerns were routinely dismissed as fringe or inconvenient. Even the most basic acts of solidarity—such as calling for a ceasefire in Gaza—were met with political cowardice from Labor and outright hostility from the Liberal–National Coalition.

Even when Israel launched one of the most brutal military assaults in recent history, killing at least 46,000 Palestinians, including thousands of children, Australia's political class refused to shift its stance. Instead, it issued weak statements about Israel's right to defend itself and repeatedly blocked even symbolic measures of support for Palestinian civilians. This unwavering support continued even as international legal bodies began investigating Israel for war crimes. No such hesitation would have existed if the situation were reversed—if an Arab state was inflicting such mass atrocities, Australia would have been at the forefront of diplomatic condemnations and sanctions.

This is not just an issue of fairness; it's an issue of democracy. A society that selectively protects one group while neglecting or demonising another is not a free society. A government that aligns itself with a powerful foreign-backed lobby at the expense of its own citizens is not acting in the national interest. And a political class that criminalised legitimate criticism while allowing real discrimination to go unaddressed was failing in its most basic responsibilities.

The reality was that this dynamic would not change by itself. The entrenched power of the Israel lobby in Australia ensured that political and media institutions would continue to serve its interests unless a serious challenge to this dominance emerged. This challenge would not come from within the political class—it would have to come from the public, from activists, from independent media, and from the communities that had been abandoned by those who claimed to represent them.

Until this changes, the message is clear: in the eyes of Australia's political establishment, some communities are worth protecting, and others are expendable. The growing anger, frustration, and disillusionment among neglected communities will not simply disappear—it will continue to build, and when it reaches a breaking point, the political class will have no one to blame but itself.

DUTTON'S DISASTER: HOW A CYCLONE EXPOSED HIS LEADERSHIP

When Cyclone Alfred appeared off the coast of Queensland in March, warnings echoed across media platforms, emergency services sprang into action and Brisbane braced itself, with authorities urging precautions and distributing sandbags. Initially classified as a serious Category 4 cyclone, Alfred weakened into a tropical low by the time it reached Queensland's coast and although it inflicted flooding and substantial rain, the damage was less catastrophic than expected and, unfortunately, this outcome provided ammunition to conspiracy theorists and right-wing pundits, eager to dismiss safety preparations as needless and "woke" measures, misrepresenting basic meteorological facts—erroneously claiming cyclones were somehow inherently less dangerous than hurricanes (in fact, cyclones, hurricanes, and typhoons are the same weather phenomena, simply named differently in various parts of the world).

As if to replicate entering the eye of the cyclone, into this unfolding drama walked Peter Dutton: initially quick to criticise and allege the federal and Queensland governments were underestimating the storm, Dutton's position soon took a politically damaging turn for the worse. Instead of remaining in his Dickson electorate—exactly where leadership visibility and empathy were urgently needed—he abruptly departed Brisbane and flew directly into a political storm of his own making. His decision: to attend an exclusive Liberal Party fundraising event in Sydney, hosted by billionaire hospitality magnate Justin Hemmes at his lavish Vaucluse mansion.

Hemmes, whose Merivale hospitality empire drew notoriety for chronic wage underpayments amounting to $19.4 million, sexual assault controversies within his venues, and even a disgraceful incident involving a video of a sexual assault at a company awards event in 2017, represented an ethical and political liability for any public official—particularly one in Dutton's position. By choosing to be seen soliciting political donations alongside Hemmes during a critical moment of crisis in his home state, Dutton committed the first major error of a series that ultimately exposed deep flaws in his political judgement and leadership abilities.

When *Sunrise* host Natalie Barr confronted him on the optics of leaving Queensland during a natural disaster to attend such a controversial fundraiser, Dutton deflected toward an attempted comparison to Labor's funding sources: "We've got a fundraiser," Dutton claimed, "I don't have the millions of dollars coming from the CFMEU and the other unions and the Prime Minister attends fundraisers". While it was true that Anthony Albanese attended a small fundraising event in Sydney on the same day as Dutton—and this is not to condone Albanese's activities—at least he was *en route* to the cyclone-affected region near Brisbane, rather than flying away from the area, as Dutton did.

Dutton then shifted blame onto Albanese and Treasurer Jim Chalmers, accusing them of exploiting a natural disaster for political gain—however, this had the opposite effect, reinforcing the perception that his priorities were misplaced and out-of-touch. As opposition leader, Dutton had both a platform and a clear opportunity to assert himself positively. As the old political saying goes, never let a good crisis go to waste.

Instead, he chose party fundraising. This decision revealed Dutton's deeper weaknesses: a failure to read the public mood, an inability to discern priorities, and a troubling comfort with aligning himself alongside ethically compromised benefactors.

Dutton also ignored a basic principle of crisis leadership clearly illustrated by his predecessor Scott Morrison. During Australia's bushfire season in 2019/20, Morrison went off to a secret holiday in Hawaii, a profound political misjudgement that ultimately ruined his prime ministership. Morrison's later mishandling of emergency funding during the 2022 Northern New South Wales floods—allocating aid selectively to politically sympathetic electorates—also highlighted the poor choice of mixing partisan politics with disaster relief. These recent examples were lessons in political mismanagement during a crisis, lessons Dutton should have understood deeply yet failed to take.

His defensive response—"I'd prefer public funding but that's how the rules are written"—did little to lessen the political damage. Instead, it amplified his perceived tone-deafness, failing to acknowledge that the rules governing political fundraising did not mandate attending exclusive events at controversial billionaires' mansions precisely when one's constituents were facing significant hardship.

This contrast between what Dutton *could have done* versus what he *actually did* opened up many questions about his leadership: that his decision-making framework was flawed and geared towards personal self-preservation and political calculation rather than genuine community need and principled leadership. The optics alone—his electorate inundated while he mixed with billionaires—would have been disastrous enough, but compounded by the ethical cloud hanging over Merivale, Dutton had essentially handed his political rivals powerful ammunition to use against him which, of course, they were now happily applying.

His misguided actions during Cyclone Alfred set off a chain reaction that reverberated powerfully, beginning with scathing public criticism, followed by growing internal party unease, declining polling, and culminating in widespread questioning of his suitability for leadership.

POLITICS BEFORE PEOPLE

The uncomfortable truth of disaster management in politics is that perception often becomes reality. Even politicians who privately lack empathy or genuine concern typically recognise the need to visibly prioritise the community's welfare during crises. Leaders didn't necessarily have to perform heroic feats or dramatically transform the outcome of a disaster, but they need to demonstrate care, empathy, and genuine concern—even if that concern for some politicians was primarily performative. Voters recognise, consciously or subconsciously, the presence of genuine empathy versus blatant opportunism, and Dutton's abrupt departure to Sydney, just hours after condemning the government's disaster response as inadequate, shattered this basic principle.

Politically, this act was reckless and indefensible. Even the simplest political instinct could have guided him towards wiser choices—where were his advisers, and what else could Dutton have done? He could have briefly visited affected communities, publicly assessing the situation and expressing solidarity, before excusing himself once satisfied that emergency services had the crisis under control. Alternatively, he could have dispatched Deputy Leader Sussan Ley—that's what deputies are for—to represent him at the fundraiser, citing pressing responsibilities at home. Such actions would have demonstrated political awareness and common sense, reinforcing the public's confidence that their leaders prioritised community safety above partisan or financial interests.

This also represented not just personal failing but a larger, structural issue within the Liberal Party (and the Liberal-National Party in Queensland). Certainly, this was just the one issue, but the persistent influence of factions and ideological rigidity has repeatedly led the Liberals to choose leaders whose political instincts are not aligned with public sentiment. The rise of community independents in traditionally Liberal electorates was a clear response to this issue and despite their philosophical alignment with core liberal principles, community independents gained traction precisely because voters felt abandoned by a party unwilling or unable to prioritise key community concerns, especially regarding climate change and environmental disasters.

Cyclone Alfred symbolised more than a weather event—it marked a growing awareness that extreme weather events were no longer rare or isolated. Climate change was reshaping expectations about disaster management, and communities demand more proactive, empathetic, and competent leadership from politicians across the spectrum. Residents of Brisbane, previously insulated from cyclone threats, now face a reality where cyclones venture further south, even reaching Coffs Harbour and potentially threatening areas once thought safe. The notion that such disasters are inherently politicised or "woke" trivialised genuine fears held by everyday Australians—voters increasingly frustrated by politicians dismissing their concerns and prioritising political advantage over decisive climate action and emergency preparedness.

The evolving threat landscape demands a new era of political leadership—one built on the fundamental understanding that disaster management must transcend partisan rivalry. Politicians need to rise above their immediate political interests and grasp the urgent reality that their communities' safety and long-term wellbeing depend on cohesive, non-partisan approaches. In failing to grasp these foundational political truths, Dutton exposed himself not merely as a poor political tactician, but as emblematic of a broader political culture that Australians were rapidly losing patience with—one which prioritised private fundraising and short-term political advantage over genuinely serving the public good.

DUTTON UNSUCCESSFULLY CHANNELLED TRUMPIAN TACTICS

Dutton's political actions also indicated a pattern of behaviour that was strongly reminiscent of Donald Trump's disruptive tactics in American politics. Mimicking Trump, Dutton often positioned himself as the political saviour, announcing unlikely solutions and outcomes that were detached from reality, even boldly declaring that he also could secure an exemption for Australia from the U.S.-imposed 25 per cent tariffs on steel and aluminium, even though no other nation had been able to achieve this. Of course, this was all possible, but was it likely? Probably not.

Much of Dutton's approach was rooted in the Trump-style belief that confidently repeated falsehoods would eventually be perceived as truths. This was apparent in his response to Cyclone Alfred, his fundraising debacle, and now the tariff issue. Yet, unlike Trump, who at least enjoyed initial success with his strategy, Dutton struggled to resonate even within his own base. His attempts at political posturing and exaggerated confidence appeared hollow, increasingly exposing him as disconnected and self-deluded rather than authoritative or inspiring. Trump's populist appeal derived from his charisma and outsider status; Dutton possessed neither—he had been a political insider for almost twenty-four years and lacked the bizarre entertainment value of Trump. Instead, his efforts to replicate Trump's rhetorical playbook amplified his shortcomings—mainly, a chronic lack of political insight and an alarming absence of genuine policy substance.

The mainstream media long asserted that Prime Minister Albanese was under sustained political pressure—which was true—and that this situation was paving the way for Dutton to win the next federal election, even to the extent of designating him as Australia's 32nd Prime Minister. However, contrary to these media assertions, it was Dutton, and not Albanese, who faced mounting political pressure, which carried through to the election campaign period, which was announced shortly after.

Even with all the support that was provided by the mainstream media, Dutton's attempts at Trumpian populism failed to gain traction. Australians largely rejected Trump's style of brash, self-centred leadership, seeing clearly through the façade. Australian politics are different to the U.S.—the political climate that enabled Trumpism in America exists on a much smaller basis in Australia, a country wary of political extremism and personality-driven politics. The electorate could be fooled sometimes, but not to this level.

Dutton's deluded self-confidence also became clearer in his misguided alignment with Trump and American Republican ideals, believing that emulating Trump's assertiveness could win over Australian voters. However, Trump's political strategy never included genuine policy coherence or international awareness. Infamously ignorant of Australian strategic assets such as Pine Gap, and even unaware of the AUKUS agreement, Trump's ignorance contrasted with Dutton's self-image as an authoritative figure on foreign policy. Dutton's belief that emulating Trump—who neither understood nor cared about Australia (which should have been obvious after the imposition of the 25 per cent tariff on Australian steel and aluminium)—could deliver him electoral success revealed profound strategic confusion and desperation.

For Australian democracy, the lesson was clear: politicians such as Dutton, who prioritised self-promotion over genuine leadership and substantive policy, inevitably failed—they might have gained some initial success, as former prime ministers Tony

Abbott and Scott Morrison did, but, ultimately, they failed. Dutton's Trumpian illusions persisted during the campaign—it was far too late to make tactical changes—and this weakened Australia's democratic discourse while undermining meaningful opposition at a critical time for the nation's political health.

THE BUDGET MYTH: HOW OUTRAGE SKEWED THE DEBATE

As Australia edged closer to the federal Budget announcement, the political atmosphere felt subdued and unusually calm—too calm for a nation whose media and political class had been addicted to economic alarmism every single day of the week. But beneath the surface, the old ideological machinery ground into gear, preparing to unleash the same tired narratives: deficits are disasters, surpluses are sacrosanct, and the only measure of economic competence is whether the Budget is in the black or red. It was as though the Australian media, in lockstep with conservative politicians, geared up to recycle the same well-worn clichés—ones that barely survived a moment of honest scrutiny.

The prevailing narrative was clear: when Labor ran a deficit—which was expected—it was cast as the end of the economic world, if not the world itself, a fiscal apocalypse borne of incompetence, recklessness, and spendthrift ideologies. However, when Labor delivered a surplus, it was brushed off as dumb luck, timing, or the favourable result of external forces well beyond their control. Conversely, when a Coalition government ran deficits—and they ran quite a few—it was always attributed to unfortunate circumstances, international headwinds, or inherited problems. And when they scraped together a surplus? It was trumpeted as the product of prudent, responsible, adult economic management, regardless of the reality.

Over the previous two years, Treasurer Jim Chalmers had quietly delivered two consecutive budget surpluses—an achievement not seen in almost two decades. He then signalled a return to deficit in the upcoming Budget, but the context mattered: it was a manageable deficit, designed to address neglected public services, essential recovery programs, and inflationary pressures without tipping the economy into stagnation. Yet this nuance was lost in the mainstream coverage, which geared up for doomsday headlines, as if Australia were hurtling toward hyperinflation or a debt spiral worthy of a banana republic.

This predictable hysteria was not just economically incoherent, it was journalistically lazy. It thrived on the financial illiteracy of much of the media commentariat—many of whom parroted phrases like "back in black" or "budget black hole" with no understanding of how macroeconomics, sovereign currency systems, or public investment work in practice. In this alternative universe, a deficit was treated as a moral failing rather than a fiscal tool, and budget policy was assessed through the lens of household accounting analogies that had no business being applied to national economies. It was economic populism dressed in the language of prudence, and it was designed to serve a political agenda, not the public good.

Chalmers was not above criticism—far from it—but compared to his recent predecessors, he appeared at least grounded in reality. He resisted the temptation to turn fiscal policy into a weapon of ideology. Instead, he focused on stabilising the Budget, reducing the structural deficit left behind by the Coalition, and targeting spending where it was needed: disaster recovery, healthcare, infrastructure, and the education sector, which had been starved of reform and funding for years. He also juggled the enormous financial weight of the AUKUS submarine deal—a geopolitical indulgence cloaked as somehow a strategic necessity, draining public funds that could otherwise have transformed domestic policy settings.

But this wasn't the conversation the electorate was offered. Instead, the national discourse was hijacked by scare campaigns and superficial talking points. Deficits are not inherently bad. In fact, in times of global economic uncertainty, they are often necessary: the Menzies government ran large budget deficits between 1958–59 and 1966–67, much larger than any deficits in the modern era, and very few commentators complained at the time. What mattered was what the money was spent on, and whether it improved national capacity, social equity, and long-term prosperity. But these questions were rarely asked on morning TV panels or in tabloid headlines. It was all about the debt.

The Budget certainly provoked a tidal wave of outrage from conservative commentators and Coalition politicians—claims of reckless spending, irresponsible governance, and impending fiscal catastrophe. But Australians had lived through nearly a decade of Coalition Budgets marked by increasing inequality, underinvestment in essential services, and economic stagnation. They remembered the real outcomes, not just the slogans. And for all the criticism Chalmers received in the following days, what he actually did was something the political system hadn't seen in a while: using economic policy to try to help people.

It still wasn't anywhere near enough but that, in itself, might have been the most radical act in that entire Budget process: putting people first, not last.

THE BUDGET AS PURE POLITICAL THEATRE

Budgets in Australia have increasingly become stage-managed political performances designed to control the media cycle for a brief moment before vanishing into the fog of public disinterest. For all the theatre, most Budgets are lucky to command a full day's attention. The Budget reply delivered by the opposition leader two nights later was even more marginalised—often broadcast during late-night shopping or up against Thursday night sport, and lost to a nation more interested in starting to think about their weekend than digesting political financial details. This short attention span has emboldened governments of all stripes to rely on drip-feed announcements in the lead-up, deploying a scattergun strategy of selective funding reveals weeks in advance, long before the Budget itself is formally tabled.

This year, there had already been announcements on boosted Medicare funding—Labor's ideological heartland—a push toward universal access to early education and childcare, support for metal and steel industries, state-targeted infrastructure spending, and funding for public education in New South Wales. These announcements blurred into one another, lacking distinction or memorability, and often appeared recycled from earlier press conferences. It became difficult to tell whether they were new initiatives, re-packaged promises, or just politically expedient reminders of previous commitments. This confusion wasn't a flaw in the strategy—it *was* the strategy, perfected by the previous Morrison government.

The Budget itself didn't necessarily introduce bold new policies or radical fiscal directions. Instead, it acted as a giant ledger, pulling together months of disparate funding measures and policy intentions into a coherent framework that could be marketed as proof of responsible governance. The message was simple: Labor had delivered targeted investments in health, education, infrastructure, and industry without blowing out the Budget or fuelling inflation. There was a deliberate contrast between these measures and the memory of a chaotic, ad-hoc Coalition era, where announcements were made for political convenience and often left unfunded or unrealised—again, a strategy perfected by Scott Morrison.

In this election year, every line item of the Budget became both a signal and a shield—signalling to the public the values and priorities of the government, while shielding it from anticipated attacks on economic management. The Coalition attempted to revive its tired trope of Labor's fiscal irresponsibility, but it fell flat in the face of Labor's recent track record—two surpluses, falling interest payments, a shrinking deficit, and visible improvements to essential services. In contrast, the Coalition still had not presented a convincing economic alternative, beyond slogans and structural opposition to public investment.

But the issue was that the entire Budget process had become an act of political choreography rather than genuine policymaking. When the Budget was treated as a public relations opportunity rather than a serious moment of economic direction-setting, the conversation stayed stuck in public image, not impact. This was especially troubling given the underlying issues that continued to plague the nation: a sluggish housing market and unaffordable rents, underemployment, stagnant wages, a still-strained health system, and an education sector—including early education—overdue for major structural reform. A few billion dollars here or there weren't going to be enough to reverse decades of systemic neglect, and there remained the lingering concern that even well-intentioned spending could be overtaken by the demands of political pragmatism.

This kind of budgeting was less about vision and more about legacy. The Albanese government wasn't just aiming for the headlines; it was aiming for permanence—of course, a government was always going to be interested in getting re-elected and remaining in office, but it had to keep sight of why it wanted to remain in office and how it could best work towards the public interest.

FANTASY FIGURES AND ECONOMIC GASLIGHTING: THE COALITION'S EXAGGERATIONS WEREN'T ENOUGH

Desperate to frame the Albanese government as fiscally irresponsible and economically destructive, the Liberal Party, through its Shadow Treasurer Angus Taylor, started throwing around the exaggerated tax claims that were designed to provoke rather than to inform. But these claims weren't just politically cynical—they were transparently false, economically incoherent, and increasingly at odds with the lived reality of most Australians.

Taylor's headline-grabbing assertion that every Australian was paying "$3,500 more in tax" since 2021—conveniently, the last year of Coalition government—wasn't just misleading; it was untraceable. There was no source, no calculation and no context, just a vague allusion to the Parliamentary Budget Office, without any of the analytical rigour or transparency one would expect from a Shadow Treasurer, and calibrated to sound just plausible enough to enrage the disengaged, while being vague enough to avoid immediate fact-checking by casual listeners.

But in this type of media environment, such laziness was reckless. If the figure was somehow based around increased tax receipts, it reflected rising incomes, stronger employment, and consumer activity—all indicators of a healthier economy. If it was based on the GST, then it was a function of more consumer spending, not government greed. Australians pay more GST when they spend more—and if they were spending more, they were generally earning more. If Taylor's data source was the tax-to-GDP ratio (which had increased), it still didn't support his narrative. That ratio was well within historical norms, and under Coalition governments, it had often been higher. In other words, whatever metric he chose—if any—it was either good economic news or bad analysis, and in this case, probably both.

The Coalition's economic messaging became a case study in political gaslighting. Taylor and his colleagues weren't attempting to engage with policy or macroeconomic reality, they were simply counting on voters to feel financially squeezed and then offering up a scapegoat—taxes—without any honest exploration of cause or context. But unlike the shock-jock era of political messaging, this kind of shallow economics didn't hold up anymore. Australians were more economically literate than the political class gave them credit for, and while they might not have gleaned through the reams of Budget papers, they certainly knew the difference between personal experience and political bluster. If their pay slips hadn't changed in the way Taylor claimed, they weren't going to swallow his talking points just because he yelled them out louder.

This was the central political problem the Coalition faced: the narrative dissonance. Political leaders couldn't keep insisting that the economy was on fire when millions of Australians were quietly noticing that—while far from perfect—the economic picture was not as dire as the Coalition claimed. Households might have felt the pinch from inflation and interest rates, but they could also see that the government had made serious investments in Medicare, early childhood education, and infrastructure. They watched as a $78 billion deficit was reduced, and they understood that patching up a decade of Coalition neglect took more than slogans and soundbites.

In that climate, trying to scare people into voting against their own experience and their own interests was a political dead-end. It was no longer enough to weaponise deficits or throw around meaningless tax claims. The modern electorate demanded specificity, realism, and—above all—honesty, and this was not something Taylor appeared capable of delivering. His *faux* theatre might have played well in media conferences or right-wing radio circles, but for a voter standing at the checkout or opening up their payslip, it was a hollow message.

Politics isn't just about who shouts the loudest: it's about whose version of reality people chose to believe. Right then, the

Coalition offered nothing more than a caricature of economic collapse, held together by dubious statistics and assumptions about voter ignorance. If they wanted to be taken seriously, they'd have to start offering something real. Until then, their economic critiques remained exactly what they appeared to be: made-up numbers, shouted into the void.

THE FEDERAL ELECTION CAMPAIGN COMMENCES

On March 28, the Prime Minister, Anthony Albanese, announced that Australia would go to the polls on May 3, with the federal election date confirmed after months of idle speculation promoted within the media—Albanese had always said that the parliament would go to the full term with an election to be held in May, and this was what came to pass. *If only the media had listened to him.* The announcement followed a big week in politics, dominated by the release of the government's Budget and the opposition's Budget reply—and both of these events fuelled more debate about tax cuts, the cost of living, and the broader direction of the country which, of course, dovetailed into the election campaign.

Treasurer Jim Chalmers essentially delivered a Budget which was aimed at stabilising the economy and offering modest cost-of-living relief. While the government promised small tax cuts and highlighted improvements in inflation and wages, this Budget was more political than visionary, designed to support the government's re-election rather than implementing bold reform. But hey, what's new?: what else could we have expected in a Budget released just a few days before the announcement of the date of the election? Chalmers insisted that the Budget laid the groundwork for a stronger economy and a better future, but it did have a lack of ambition on issues such as corporate tax reform and environmental protections.

As was to be expected for a pre-election Budget, there were sweeteners for voters but no radical changes. Major corporations, especially in the mining and gas sectors, continued to benefit from a slack tax regime, with little indication of any reform in the near future. The idea of taxing windfall profits from the minerals and resources that are owned by all of us—and a source of revenue for public investment—remained untouched, despite the calls from economists and community leaders for a more equitable system. These were not new ideas: the Henry Review from 2010—commissioned by the then Labor government—contained all of these good reforms; if only someone from the government could have been bothered to look for it.

The opposition's Budget reply, delivered by Peter Dutton—with a supporting role from Shadow Treasurer Angus Taylor—did very little to create any enthusiasm for any economic reform that might have been in the public interest. They rejected the government's tax cuts—an unusual political move so close to an election and one which would cost them so dearly during the campaign—arguing the measures were a "cruel hoax" and not enough to address Australia's allegedly declining living standards. The Coalition instead proposed halving the fuel excise for a year, a populist measure that was likely to benefit oil companies more than consumers and reduce revenues for the government. Their broader policy platform remained vague, focusing on cutting public service jobs—the number of which continued to creep up: 36,000 the previous week, 41,000 the next—and pursuing nuclear energy, a proposal driven by mining magnate Gina Rinehart, and driven more by political theatre than any practical solutions.

Despite the government being a disappointment from a progressive perspective—environmental backsliding and new coal mines and gas fields, weak higher education reform, and its muted response to the complete destruction of Gaza—the polls continued to favour the Labor government. Albanese's leadership had always been presented and promoted as cautious—and while this caution limited the amount of progressive change that occurred during this parliamentary term, the prime minister never promised anything else but caution, and he delivered on this in spades—and this appeared to resonate with voters more than Dutton's erratic and negative campaigning. Labor's successes, such as lower inflation and wage growth, were downplayed by the mainstream media and didn't generate headline-grabbing moments, but this offered a steady alternative to the Coalition's volatile pitch. And at a time of global uncertainty and an increasingly chaotic and dysfunctional regime in the United States, this might have been the main feature that the electorate was looking for.

Climate change, once a central theme of Labor's 2022 campaign, barely featured in 2025's pre-election discussions, and didn't feature very much during the campaign. The government's mixed record on the environment and climate change—including opening new coal and gas projects and scrapping plans for the Environmental Protection Authority—drew fire from environmental groups and independents. Meanwhile, community independents and the Australian Greens continued to raise issues such as environmental protection and mining royalties, pressuring both major parties to address long-ignored structural problems.

On international issues, Albanese's invitation to U.S. President Donald Trump was a strange choice, to say the least. While any visit—if the invitation was taken up by Trump—was likely to be scheduled after the election, it sent an odd message at a time when many global leaders were distancing themselves from the U.S. On foreign affairs, the government maintained support for Ukraine, but its silence on the humanitarian crisis in Palestine continued to attract criticism from many progressives and from within Labor ranks.

Did Palestine become an issue during the election campaign? There was some electoral effect in western Sydney and parts of outer Melbourne: it was difficult to know what would happen at that time—many Islamic communities are loyal to the Labor Party and wouldn't necessarily have voted for an independent candidate just because they were from an Islamic background, such as Ziad Basyouny in the seat of Watson, but we just didn't know what type of effect the issue of Palestine was going to have in these areas and, ultimately, the effect was negligible.

Indigenous affairs, too, appeared to be sidelined within the Budget and were avoided during the election campaign—there just aren't enough votes in Indigenous issues for the mainstream parties and if there was to be any effect, it was likely to have come from the Liberal and National parties, who would have been happy to use these issues as a political wedge, following on from their racist tactics that were used during the failed Voice to Parliament referendum in 2023. Indeed, the final week of the campaign saw the Coalition strongly campaigning on the idea that Labor was going to re-introduce the Voice to Parliament by stealth—but this had little effect on the final election result.

With polls at the time leaning toward a narrow Labor victory or even a minority government supported by independents and the Greens, the election outcome could have hinged on how effectively the government responded to calls for real reform. Many voters appeared to be seeking a return to more ambitious, values-driven governance that resembled those of past Labor reformers like Whitlam, Hawke, and Keating. But whether this government was prepared—or willing—to rise to that challenge seemed unlikely.

LABOR'S MOMENTUM AND A SHAKY START FOR THE COALITION

The opening days of the federal election campaign revealed more than just policy announcements and talking points—they exposed a difference between a government that appeared match fit and ready to go, and an opposition still fumbling around and trying to find its balance. While the early parts of any campaign are marked by adjustments and recalibration—it was only day four of a thirty-six-day campaign—one major party hit the ground running, and it wasn't the Coalition. Of course, there was always a feeling that it could have changed—but it was a big concern that Peter Dutton seemed so unprepared. Prime Minister Anthony Albanese didn't call an early or a snap election and the final date that the election could be held was always going to be May 17—two weeks after the actual date that was announced—so this lack of preparation came as a surprise.

Albanese made a confident start to the campaign, with a populist pitch targeting the supermarket giants—Coles and Woolworths—that many in the electorate had become increasingly resentful of. By promising to outlaw price gouging and create mechanisms to penalise excessive profiteering, Labor tried to boost its cost-of-living credentials and positioned itself as a defender of everyday consumers. Albanese's rhetoric of accusing supermarkets of "taking the piss" wasn't trying to be deliberately crude, but it was politically calculated. At least a sweary Albanese and a willingness to be aggressive, populist and blunt in language, cut through the abstraction that often grinds federal election campaigns down, where everyone tries to be the most inoffensive and obtuse. And this was one message the prime minister wanted to put out: Labor would take on the corporate giants, whereas the Coalition would not.

On the other side of the political fence, Dutton's start was marked by disarray and rhetorical backflips. Over the first few days, he floated the possibility of two separate referendums—four-year parliamentary terms, and stripping dual nationals of citizenship—only to backflip quickly, and this followed on from the constitutional recognition of Indigenous people that he promised in 2023, only to retract that proposal as well. It's always difficult for oppositions to be fully prepared for an election that is the prerogative of the Prime Minister to call, but even still, it was a sign that the Coalition had not properly war-gamed or been grounded in a unified message.

The confusion continued into other policy areas, particularly around the Coalition's gas plan. Dutton made bold claims about reducing gas prices through a form of domestic reservation, forcing Queensland producers to divert up to 100 additional petajoules to the east coast. Aside from the difficulties of trying to announce and debate the esoteric issues of petajoules to the electorate, neither the modelling nor the mechanics of this proposal were released.

LABOR'S MOMENTUM AND A SHAKY START FOR THE COALITION

Former ACCC chair Rod Sims led the criticism, pointing out the flaws and impracticalities in this plan, while the Minister for Climate Change and Energy, Chris Bowen, accused Dutton of "making it up as he goes". The absence of economic detail, industry backing, or a coherent regulatory strategy weakened what could have been a centrepiece cost-of-living pitch for the Coalition. It looked instead like a reactive move: a bid to grab relevance in a news cycle, rather than shape it—it's possible to get away with this type of approach for most parts of a parliamentary term but during an election campaign, it put out the message that the Coalition was just not ready to return to office.

It wasn't just the policy vacuums that hurt Dutton—it was the tone and posture. For most of that parliamentary term, Dutton avoided direct scrutiny, seeking media opportunities with right-wing commentators and Coalition-friendly journalists and he then found himself exposed in the spotlight of a national election campaign. There was nowhere to hide during an election campaign. Albanese, for the first few days at least, appeared more comfortable, shaping the campaign narrative early with a confident media presence. Dutton, in contrast, appeared flat-footed, reactive and unconvincing.

While it was far too early to claim that the election result was all over, the early optics mattered and set the tone for the campaign. And at that point, the Coalition presented itself as unprepared, fractured, and searching for a message. The published opinion polls began to reflect this sentiment, with little indication that Dutton was making meaningful inroads into Labor's lead.

THE POLLS SHOWED A CHANGE IN THE ELECTORATE

In late March, a series of opinion polls—the Morgan Poll showing 53–47 per cent to Labor in two-party-preferred voting, YouGov, Newspoll and Resolve all giving Labor a 51–49 per cent lead—continued with a pattern that commenced just over a month before: the electorate was moving towards the government. While no single poll was definitive, the cumulative picture was one of a campaign drifting away from the opposition at precisely the moment it needed to be gaining traction.

Betting markets started to reflect this reality too, with odds shortening in Labor's favour: these markets should have been ignored though and are quite often incorrect—betting agencies paid out early on Bill Shorten winning in 2019, only for Scott Morrison to go and win the election—but they did reflect some sentiment within the community, or at least those who were prepared to part with their money in a volatile betting market. These early trends didn't guarantee a Labor victory, but they signalled trouble for the Coalition.

For most of that parliamentary term, Albanese was a cautious, defensive prime minister but he embraced a sharper, more confident position on the campaign trail—and perhaps Albanese was a far better campaigner than he was as prime minister and it was something they would need to address in the future.

In exchanges with the media—asked irrelevant questions by Sky News' Simon Love (about the removal of a Liberal Party sign by the husband of the independent MP, Monique Ryan)—Albanese highlighted the absurdity of the question and the triviality of the media's priorities. In another exchange with ABC journalist Patricia Karvelas, where she falsely claimed that Infrastructure

LABOR'S MOMENTUM AND A SHAKY START FOR THE COALITION

Australia had deemed Victoria's Suburban Rail Loop project unviable, Albanese called her out and set the record straight. Why had Albanese waited so long to push back against the endless attacks and mistruths spoken to him by the mainstream media? And, perhaps more importantly, why did the media always get things wrong or just make stuff up?

The contrast with Dutton couldn't have been more different: increasingly low-energy, jittery, defensive, reactive and arrogant. His early campaign stumbles—the confused messaging around proposed referendums and a half-baked gas plan—already sowed doubt about his preparedness. But it was his tone that stood out: not assertive, not energised, but desperate. In media appearances, Dutton relied on recycled attacks on Labor's cost-of-living management and when challenged, leaned into old tropes about negative campaigns from the Labor Party and media bias—not the behaviour of a leader with a compelling case for change and trying to govern for all people.

And then there was the issue in Dutton's seat: the electorate of Dickson had always been marginal, but that time it was targeted not just by Labor's Ali France, but by a rising community independent, Ellie Smith, who gained traction among voters disillusioned with both major parties. That Dutton might have been forced to fight for his political survival and spend more time in his own seat, while trying to sell himself as a future prime minister was a major disadvantage, and he probably knew it. It was rare for an opposition leader or senior minister to be facing a real risk of losing their own seat in an election campaign—he only needed to refer to the difficulties the former Treasurer Josh Frydenberg had in trying to spread a message on the national stage, but holed up in Kooyong during the 2022 election campaign, trying to hold on to the seat which he ultimately lost to Monique Ryan.

Because of his insulation from media scrutiny, three days into the campaign, Dutton was already being tested in ways the previous three years had not. For all the assistance offered by the conservative press, from Sky News to *The Australian* to sections of the ABC (for all of Sunday on ABC News 24, Dutton's appearances and mentions outnumbered Albanese by a ratio of 2:1)—Dutton still struggled to connect and the more voters saw of him, the less convinced they seemed to be, which was what the opinion polls were suggesting.

In politics, self-belief is critical. Leaders need to exude not just confidence, but purpose. At that moment, Dutton's campaign felt like it was missing both. Where once there may have been a longer-term strategy for the Coalition—lose the 2025 election, gain ground, then mount a serious challenge in 2028—there was now visible panic. The spring in his step was gone, replaced with a sense of clinging on, not surging forward. Dutton had always been a front-runner and once he started struggling and fell behind, he didn't display the energy of a government-in-waiting; it was more the actions of a man on borrowed political time.

Of course, campaigns can always turn. Momentum can shift. Scandals could erupt, and established narratives could easily fall apart. In the 1993 federal election, the Coalition led by 53 to 47 per cent in the two-party preferred vote on the first day of that campaign—even holding a five-point buffer in the final week—only to lose on election day. And in a reflection of the 1993 election, the Labor Party lost the 2019 election, after leading nearly every opinion poll after the 2016 election. Things could always change, and the opinion polls could sometimes be wrong.

But with each passing day, it became harder to see how the Coalition could gain the support it needed to win majority government, or even position itself credibly as a minority government. The idea that this was going to be a 'close-run contest' in the parlance of horse-race journalism, and as many in the media suggested, fast evaporated. And while Dutton might still have believed in his chances, belief alone didn't win elections—traction did. And right then, after the first week of the campaign, Dutton and the Coalition just weren't getting it.

DUTTON'S DISASTROUS START TO THE CAMPAIGN

The first week of the federal election campaign ended, and what became immediately clear was just how under-prepared, incoherent, and self-destructive the Liberal Party appeared to be under Peter Dutton's leadership. What should have been an opportunity to showcase discipline, vision, and a credible alternative to the Labor government instead became a case study in political mismanagement. From tone-deaf gaffes to rhetoric designed to inflame the public, the Coalition's opening week revealed a party that was out of touch, stuck in an echo chamber and a cul-de-sac of outdated culture wars, and unable to articulate a compelling agenda for the country.

Dutton, who had been expected to use this campaign to reframe his public image and project leadership potential—or a chance to "smile and maybe show a different side" and the rest of his character, as he had said in his challenge against then Prime Minister, Malcolm Turnbull in 2018—only reinforced the perception of a figure out of step with the electorate.

His fallback on tired old tropes—China fear-mongering, accusations of 'indoctrination" in school education, the anti-'woke' rhetoric—made him appear trapped in the past, and not opening up to the future. These tactics might have stirred up parts of the conservative base, but they appeared tone-deaf to a broader electorate searching for optimism and clarity. Leaders who wanted to win elections needed to appeal to a wider audience, not just the conservative rump of their own party who argued the pathway to victory would be assured, if only the Liberal Party could become even more right wing.

Meanwhile, the Coalition bungled its response to the big trade issue of the week: the 10 per cent tariff imposed by the United States on Australian goods. Rather than offering a considered response, Dutton reached for the populist megaphone, insisting that he would have secured an exemption—despite the fact that no country achieved this under the new U.S. trade measures, not even the Heard and McDonald Islands, Australian territory which was uninhabited by humans, but populated with penguins and many other birds, wildlife and sea creatures. These were empty talking points in place of substance, another example of a campaign more interested in grievance and outrage than governance.

Then came the comments about official residences: Dutton declared he would have preferred to live in Kirribilli House in Sydney rather than The Lodge in Canberra if elected Prime Minister, dissing the people of Canberra at the same time. In the midst of a national housing crisis, the optics were terrible. To voters struggling with rising rents and home ownership out of reach, a prospective leader appearing to pick and choose between luxury homes was not just out of touch—it was insulting—as if to suggest that the position of prime minister for Dutton was going to become a procession of holidays in a harbour-side mansion. Certainly, these were just minor issues but they provided insight into the lack of discipline within the Coalition's campaign.

Compounding all of this were growing reports of internal disunity. The continuing leaks from the New South Wales division of the Liberal Party suggested that moderates were actively working against the leadership, even supplying information directly to the Labor Party. It was a clear sign of the discontent brewing within the ranks, as the moderate faction of New South Wales sought to wrest back control from the conservative Queensland rump.

By the end of the first week, Dutton looked like a man stumbling through a minefield of his own making. The campaign was supposed to be his moment to prove he could lead the nation. Instead, he delivered panic, provocation and, above all, a constant stream of negativity. The Coalition had a chance to reset and offer a real alternative but what it offered instead, was chaos. They squibbed it.

THE OPINION POLL NUMBERS FALLING FOR THE COALITION

At the end of this first week, across every major opinion poll, the trend was consistent and a pattern formed: voters drifted away from the Coalition and speculations and feelings about this drift were confirmed by numbers. The figures suggested that Dutton and the Liberal Party were heading for a disaster on election day.

Four major polls—Roy Morgan, Essential, Resolve and Freshwater—were released during the week, and while the figures were all slightly different, all pointed to a clear loss of momentum for the Coalition. The most influential opinion poll, Newspoll, released late on the Sunday night, painted an even more difficult picture for the Liberal Party: 52 per cent to Labor and 48 per cent to the Coalition on a two-party-preferred basis, which was similar to the results of the 2022 federal election. While a four-point gap may have seemed surmountable, in the context of federal elections, it could spell the difference between a marginal loss and a complete rout.

Despite the cliché of the only poll that matters is the poll on election day, the hard heads in the respective campaign strategy teams would have known that these trends did matter. Polls taken in aggregate don't just tell who is ahead at any given time; they reveal where momentum is building, the messages that are resonating, and where all the vulnerabilities lay. And at that time, the data suggested Dutton's campaign was repelling more voters than it was attracting, especially women.

Pollsters have a vested interest in accuracy, especially when it gets much closer to the date of the election. While some may have had ideological biases and interpret the results to support political agendas outside of the election period, their business model depends on being taken seriously so close to when the real result—the actual election—is revealed. So, when every opinion poll showed the same pattern, it became impossible to ignore: the Liberal–National Coalition was in serious trouble.

EVEN SKY NEWS STARTED TO TURN AWAY

One of the more telling moments of the week—albeit small—came not from a politician, but from the Coalition's unofficial media wing. On Sky News—long regarded as the centre of conservative spin—even the propaganda machine seemed to have had enough. In a series of vox pops conducted in Melbourne, voters offered their views on the party leaders, and rather than cherry-picking favourable responses, Sky aired raw, unfiltered public sentiment—and it didn't favour Dutton.

Asked about Albanese, voters described him as "doing a good job" or "okay". When Dutton's name came up, the reactions were quick: "He's not that popular"... "No" ..."I don't think he'll do good". For a network known for its editorial manipulations and fabrications at every opportunity, this was a deviation from the script, and definitely not on message. Not that too many people watch Sky News, but it does have a dedicated hardcore audience, addicted to conservative bias and the politics of outrage, just like its big brother in the U.S., Fox News. Whether intentional or accidental, this signalled a rare admission: the public wasn't buying what the Coalition was selling.

THE BIGGER QUESTION IS: WHY WASN'T THE COALITION READY FOR THIS CAMPAIGN?

Everyone knew the election had to be called by May 17 at the latest and even if the actual date—May 3—wasn't known, there would have been an expectation after the summer break in late January, that an election would have to be called soon. Yet the Liberals began the campaign caught off guard, unsure of their footing. The messaging lacked cohesion, their agenda appeared thin, and their overall tone reeked of complacency and incompetence.

In contrast, Labor looked disciplined, prepared and confident. Perhaps learning from the Voice to Parliament referendum, where the 'No' side mobilised early and seized the agenda, Albanese's team struck early and decisively. Of course, they knew exactly when the election was going to be called, but they framed the campaign even before Dutton knew what was going on.

While Dutton obviously borrowed from Trump's chaos campaign playbook—by projecting disorder and chaos to conceal strategies that might have arrived later in the campaign (or even policies announced after the election was over)—it was a tactic that didn't translate into Australian politics. Although there have been a small number of instances of voter fraud, double voting and electoral manipulation in Australia, there is not enough of it to influence election outcomes—our electoral system is too robust, too transparent, and too decentralised to allow chaos to become a campaign strategy. And besides this, Dutton had neither the charisma nor the ability to pull it off. As much as he'd like to try, he was not Donald Trump.

With opinion polling numbers becoming more set, internal divisions widening, and the public losing interest, the early warning signs turned into alarm bells. Even the Coalition's staunchest media allies started to back away—Sky News but, interestingly, not the ABC—if only subtly. When the echo chamber started to crack like this, it was often a sign of the entire edifice beginning to collapse.

At this stage, there were still just under four weeks remaining in the 2025 election campaign and anything could have happened in these final weeks. A five-point lead in the opinion polls evaporated for opposition leader John Hewson in the 1993 federal election and he lost that election, even though just the day before the election, the Liberal Party was still highly expected to win. That was a surprise victory, as was the 2019 federal election, which was lost by the Labor Party. If the Dutton-led Coalition had somehow won the 2025 election, it would have been a genuine surprise election victory, and these types of surprise victories tend to only happen once in a generation. Week one of this campaign was supposed to set the tone. Instead, it exposed fragility, lack of preparation, and a deep disconnect between Dutton and the electorate.

THE ELECTION FEAR AND PARANOIA CIRCUS ACT

It was still the early stages of the federal election campaign, but the Coalition had already reached for one of its oldest and most divisive tools: China. Lacking substantive policy ideas or credible achievements to highlight, the opposition once again dipped into that vast pool of nationalist paranoia, this time targeting a Chinese research vessel that *legally* passed through international waters.

The ship, part of a joint scientific project with New Zealand, was navigating between Victoria and Tasmania—a voyage through lawful maritime zones. Prime Minister Anthony Albanese initially sought a measured tone, acknowledging the ship's presence and confirming it was under surveillance by the Australian Defence Force. Then came the unnecessary concession that he "wished it wasn't there at all," a vague statement that gave Peter Dutton the opportunity to whip up a frenzy, yet again.

Dutton wastes no time when it come to these opportunities to race bait and so it turned out to be in this case. Abandoning the facts in favour of base racism, he accused the Prime Minister of having "lost control" of national security, and claimed—without any evidence—that the vessel was gathering intelligence and mapping undersea cables critical to Australia's communications. This innocuous research ship, in Dutton's imagination, became a Chinese spy ship, an invisible threat hovering off the coast. The media followed suit—of course—amplifying the panic with sensationalist speculation about sabotage and espionage.

At the Prime Minister's media conference, journalists' aggressive questions reflected this media-fuelled hysteria: What was the ship researching? What had been done to protect our undersea infrastructure? Had anything been communicated to the Chinese government? Albanese maintained a cautious line amid all this paranoia, reaffirming Australia's commitment to monitoring foreign vessels and respecting international law. But by then, the narrative had already shifted. In the public domain, the ship had been transformed from a benign research vessel into a symbol of Chinese aggression—not due to facts, but to political opportunism—and that the entire 27 million people of Australia, and the massive 33,000 kilometres of coastline were somehow going to be breached and seriously under threat.

This episode spoke volumes about Australian politics and very little about China's actual behaviour, as well as showing how a complex issue could be reduced to a simple fear campaign. The truth—that it was a joint mission with one of our closest allies—barely made a mention in any of the media coverage. Perhaps Albanese could have clearly stated that China was Australia's largest trading partner and a good friend to this country, instead of saying he wished the ship "wasn't there at all". This might have diffused the hysteria somewhat, but the reality was, Dutton would have found a way to escalate this issue regardless.

Dutton's goal had been simple: to dominate the media cycle after a poor start to the election campaign and reassert the Liberal Party's supposed strength on national security—despite a history marked by foreign policy blunders, underfunded cyber defences, and international embarrassment.

And so, the national conversation during the election campaign had been hijacked by an invented crisis. Instead of discussing real issues—climate, healthcare, housing, the cost of living—the country was fixated on a small research ship in international waters. Why? Because fear of China was an easy distraction, as it always had been throughout Australia's history, the race card the Coalition played so well, and the media never hesitated to endorse.

THE RED SCARE AND ANTI-CHINA HYSTERIA REARED ITS UGLY HEAD AGAIN

There was something disturbingly familiar about the way Australia erupts into panic whenever China appears in domestic political debates. It took very little: a research ship with Mandarin signage on its bow, a shipping log, a blurry photo, or a vague military report. Once triggered, the machinery of hysteria sprang into action—politicians manufactured outrage, and the media amplified it with alarmist speculation. The result was rarely rooted in fact, but in cultural anxiety, residual racism, and an enduring Cold War mentality.

The Coalition had perfected this playbook. It had used it time and again—against asylum seekers, against Huawei, Chinese universities, international students, the Belt and Road Initiative, and finally, against a modest research vessel scanning the ocean floors providing important scientific research on crustacea and other sea creatures, in conjunction with a trusted partner in New Zealand. And the plot never changes: China was *infiltrating*, China was *spying*, China was *coming for us*. The yellow peril; the red peril... China was always in the wrong, Australia was always right. Each rewrite of this story adjusted the volume and the visuals, but the message stayed the same.

This engineered xenophobia wasn't accidental; it was strategic. By portraying China as a looming threat, Dutton distracted from the economic issues and his own political performances. And the media, complicit in this game, obliged with headlines, maps, and dire hypotheticals.

Rarely did the media challenge this narrative. China was not treated as a complex nation of 1.4 billion people with a multifaceted relationship with Australia. Instead, it became a caricature for everything the political class wished to externalise: fear, uncertainty, and the unknown. The *other*. Somehow, China was both our largest trading partner and our gravest national threat. This contradiction was never resolved because it didn't have to be: fear would always work.

And this was a contradiction deeply embedded in Australia's identity. From the "yellow peril" hysteria of the nineteenth century to the communist Asian invasion myths of the twentieth century, fear of China had long been part of the national psyche. The 2025 media cycle just gave it new packaging—a rebranding for an old prejudice.

But the consequences were real. This political theatre undermined Australia's international reputation, it alienated

Chinese–Australian communities, and reduced complex global issues to empty slogans. It trivialised legitimate concerns—such as China's human rights record—by folding them into cheap domestic point-scoring. It also revealed a nation pretending to be a Pacific leader while behaving like a regional backwater bathing in its own racist ineptitude.

Certainly, China's authoritarianism deserves criticism, there's no question about this. Its record on civil liberties, its aggressive diplomacy, and its treatment of minorities should concern us and the international community. But reacting with hysteria instead of diplomacy only weakened Australia's credibility. We didn't need to choose between appeasement and paranoia: we just needed to grow up.

If Australia wanted to act like a middle power, it needed to stop behaving like a fearful outpost, a baby country in the style of a mini-me United States. Calm, mature leadership was not weakness. Trade was not betrayal. And diplomacy required more than slogans shouted from within the Canberra bubble.

HOW DUTTON'S CAMPAIGN STARTED TO FALL APART

The second week of the federal election campaign—a stage when political parties sought stability—descended into yet more misfires for the Liberal Party, and it started off with bringing one of the worst deals in recent political history into the campaign: the lease in 2015 of the Port of Darwin to a Chinese company, the Landbridge Group. Despite having implemented the entire deal, the Coalition sought to reframe the issue as a national security threat in an attempt to reignite anti-China sentiment and regain some control over their campaign.

Peter Dutton had been scheduled to announce the cancellation of the lease as part of this scare campaign, but the move backfired spectacularly. Labor—tipped off through yet another leak directly from the Liberal Party—pre-empted the announcement, with Anthony Albanese revealing a near-identical policy the day before. It wasn't just a political embarrassment—it completely nullified the issue. What had been meant to be a moment of nationalistic megaphoning for the Coalition became an echo of the government's position, with Dutton left to agree with a plan that had been in the public domain for less than twenty-four hours. Worse still, the very issue the Coalition had tried to weaponise reminded voters that it was actually the Coalition who had signed off on this poor deal in the first place.

The Coalition's attempt to magnify this into yet another chapter from their now-familiar China scare campaign exposed the big contradiction at the heart of their message: how could a nation's largest trading partner also be its greatest security threat? It wasn't an existential question—if China really had been that threatening, why sell or lease major infrastructure to Chinese companies in the first place?

THE HYPOCRISY AT THE HEART OF THE PORT OF DARWIN LEASE

Nothing better illustrated the performative nature of Australia's national security politics than the saga of the Port of Darwin. In 2015, during the time the Coalition was in office, the Northern Territory's Country Liberal Party government leased the port to the Landbridge Group—a deal proposed by the territory government, approved at the federal level and quietly welcomed by Coalition insiders.

It was a ninety-nine-year lease at a price of just $506 million (or a bargain price of $5 million per year), with no serious scrutiny or strategic foresight. Even worse, former Liberal Party Trade Minister Andrew Robb took an $800,000 consulting role with Landbridge immediately after leaving Parliament—and possibly before his exit—a clear conflict of interest that stank so severely of impropriety. At the time, there had been minimal media outrage. No national security alarm bells.

Ten years later in 2025, the Port of Darwin had become a political football, with both major parties pledging to unwind the lease in the name of national sovereignty. The Coalition, eager to rewrite history, conveniently erased its role in the deal, positioning itself as the defender of Australian interests. The media, once again, helped out in this narrative sleight of hand.

Labor, instead of challenging this revisionism, followed suit—framing its own reversal as a bipartisan act of national interest. But there was no acknowledgement of the systemic failures that allowed the lease in the first place: a decade of shortsightedness, transactional politics, and elite self-enrichment.

The port became a stage prop in a broader election narrative—used to project strength, distract from economic stagnation, and reinforce anti-China sentiment. Yet there had been no evidence of any security breach or strategic failure arising from the lease and, from all accounts, Landbridge proved to be a good operator of the port. The optics, not the facts, drove the calls to reclaim the port. And Landbridge held all the cards: if there was to be a 'just compensation' under the terms of the contract, the company would receive far more than the $506 million it agreed to pay in 2015.

It was so typical of Australian governments: a poor deal on gas in 2005 meant that the country ended up buying its own gas back from markets in China, Japan and South Korea at an inflated consumer price, a ridiculous situation created by the Howard government but continued by Labor governments, and this would continue until at least 2032. Iron ore sold to overseas interests at a low price, and most of the profits going to mining magnates such as Gina Rinehart, Andrew Forrest or multinational entities, with little in royalties returned to the Commonwealth of Australia. Governments agreed to this.

And now, a likely large compensation package to a Chinese-owned company to lease back the Port of Darwin. To use the parlance of Kerry Packer when he sold the Nine Network to Alan Bond at an inflated price of $1 billion in 1987, only to buy it back several years later at a quarter of the sale price, the Chinese government would be thinking: *You only get one Australian government in your lifetime, and we've had ours.*

This was the core contradiction at the heart of Australia's China policy. China was only a threat when politically convenient. When donations flowed, jobs were created, or marginal seats were in play, China became a valued partner. But when an election neared, the same relationships were rebranded as national security threats. It was the classic behaviour of a racist nation: we're all mates when you do as you're told and behave in the way we expect you to behave. Reclaiming the Port of Darwin could well have been the right decision in the national interest. It did seem peculiar for the government in 2015 to be leasing the port to any foreign interests but also in the way that it produced such a bad financial deal for the Northern Territory government. But it didn't undo the damage of a political culture that sold out national infrastructure for short-term gain—and now expected applause for pretending to fix it.

THE LIBERAL PARTY'S CIVIL WAR

This focus on the Port of Darwin hadn't just been about national infrastructure or foreign policy. It had been about the cynical recycling of fear for political gain—and this time, it didn't work. Labor outflanked them—ironically, with the direct help of a leak from some unhappy people within the Liberal Party. This party leak to the Labor Party hadn't come from an external source or accidentally found in a discarded filing cabinet on the outskirts of Canberra. It had come directly from the Liberal Party, and all signs pointed to the New South Wales branch as the saboteur. It was the result of a long-standing power struggle between the more ideologically conservative Liberal–National Party of Queensland—Dutton's base—and the moderates of New South Wales, who would prefer to see their own ascendancy after an election defeat, even if that meant handing Labor the win.

This isn't a new dynamic in Australian politics, but rarely had it played out so obviously in the middle of a federal campaign. Behind the scenes, the New South Wales branch—hardly a pinnacle of liberal moderation itself—had increasingly prepared the ground for an Angus Taylor or Sussan Ley leadership in the event of a Coalition loss. For them, losing in 2025 would be an acceptable price to pay for retaking control of the party, silencing the Queensland-led hard-right, and charting a new direction that could win in 2028 or beyond. If Dutton were to lose his own seat of Dickson in the process—which ended up being the case—that would be an added benefit.

And while it might have seemed counterintuitive to sabotage their own campaign, political operatives often viewed factional victory within the party as more important than electoral success—especially when the electoral odds already looked grim. The Labor Party has had a strong tendency to do this in the past, and its greatest act of factional bastardry had to be the period between 2010–13, when it destroyed itself during the Rudd–Gillard–Rudd years, and handed the Liberal Party a nine-year period of government on a plate.

Dutton had clearly been aware of this internal bleeding. His complaints during the campaign about "elites within the Liberal Party" weren't random grievances—they had been directed at the very people who were undermining him. Yet this public airing of these internal grievances had done little to stop the quiet campaign against him. The New South Wales branch hadn't been without its problems: its leadership was fragmented, its ideological direction confused, and while it hadn't been the far-right circus that the Victorian branch had become—now home to Christian nationalists and conspiracy theorists—it still harboured its own internal instability.

A MID-CAMPAIGN POLICY DUMP

To add to his terrible week, Dutton's abrupt abandonment of the Coalition's plan to force public servants back into the office full-time had been less a policy correction than a public confession of political incompetence. In a rare display of a campaign apology, Dutton had openly admitted the policy was a mistake and tried to frame it as a case of miscommunication—blaming Labor for twisting the message, as though the policy hadn't already collapsed under its own contradictions. In reality, this hadn't been a complex or nuanced idea misrepresented by opponents— it had been a shambles from the beginning. Announced with great fanfare to appeal to a supposed silent majority of tradies and working-class voters tired of 'lazy' remote workers, it had quickly unravelled under the weight of its own impracticality, potential illegality, and hypocrisy.

The sudden backflip hadn't happened because the policy was debated, articulated over time and then found wanting: it had happened because voters hated it. It alienated not only the public servants it directly targeted but also their families, colleagues, and entire segments of the electorate who had come to see remote work as an essential part of modern life. The Coalition's attempt to pit 'real workers' against 'keyboard loafers' collapsed when it became clear that many of those 'real workers' relied on the flexibility of their partners, family members, or housemates working from home.

This flip-flop confirmed what had already been suspected: the Coalition's policy platform had been hastily put together, poorly vetted, and driven more by political messaging than any real belief in this platform. Dumping the work-from-home policy in the middle of a campaign had sent a message to the electorate—not that the party was being responsive to public sentiment, but that it had been unprepared. And worse still, it gave Labor and independents a line of attack that endured for the rest of the campaign: if the Coalition was already disowning its own policies, how could voters trust anything else they promised?

Ultimately, this hadn't just been about one failed idea. It raised a broader question about the Coalition's readiness for government. What other policies hadn't been tested? What else might have collapsed under scrutiny? Nuclear energy? Education reform? Taxation? There had been a growing sense that the Coalition, out of government for only three years, hadn't done the hard policy work in opposition and was only relying on outdated ideas and cynical stunts. And that might have been the most damning conclusion of all: a party that once could win by simply showing up, now faced a political world that demanded a great deal more—and it didn't have much to offer.

HOW DUTTON'S CAMPAIGN STARTED TO FALL APART

LEADERSHIP IN THE AGE OF TALKING POINTS

The first leadership debate of the federal election campaign appeared during this week—a tightly managed exercise in message control more than any genuine contest of ideas. Albanese and Dutton had stood before a studio audience of 100 'undecided' voters and delivered performances that had been technically competent but left no lasting impression, with each sticking to their pre-packaged talking points. Albanese rattled off economic achievements, Dutton leaned into cost-of-living anxieties, and the entire event felt like a well-rehearsed dress rehearsal for a show no one particularly wanted to see.

While Albanese won the debate with 44 per cent, to Dutton's 35 per cent—21 per cent remained undecided—there had been no real persuasion, no momentum gained. It had just been another night in a campaign going through the motions.

But the problem ran deeper than just an uninspiring debate. It was what these debates had become—tightly managed performances with no spontaneity, no improvisation, and no real test of leadership under pressure. They were relics of a past political culture that demanded less but offered more, where decades ago, political leaders faced unruly, unpredictable crowds and had to sink or swim in real time. Today's debates had been risk-managed into irrelevance.

It was hard to imagine either Albanese or Dutton confronting a crowd not handpicked by a research firm, let alone dealing with hecklers or winning over a room determined to dislike them. The oratory that once defined great Australian leaders had been replaced by scriptwriters and communications consultants. Politics now happened within the safe walls of subscription media and strategic messaging, not out in the open, where views were tested and leaders either rose or fell on the strength of their character. The electorate deserved to see leaders tested in a way that wasn't choreographed within an inch of its life. The current format taught us nothing and challenged no one.

And so, we were left with debates that confirmed, rather than challenged. They confirmed the instinct of many Australians that their leaders didn't really say anything anymore. They confirmed that politics had become more about avoiding damage than taking risks. And they confirmed that, in a campaign where leadership was supposedly at stake, neither contender wanted to be caught off guard. But the real tragedy is that without risk, there is no inspiration—and without inspiration, there's no leadership worth following.

FOOTBALLS AND FOSSIL FUELS

Every election campaign has its unscripted moments, and these unexpected incidents revealed more about a leader's temperament and values than any carefully rehearsed debate or media conference. In this week, two such moments had stood out—small but significant in their symbolism. The first involved Dutton, a football, and a cameraman; the other saw Albanese confronted by a climate change activist. Neither moment decided the election, but the respective reactions said a lot about the politics they represented.

At a photo-op on a football field, Dutton managed to kick a ball directly into the head of a cameraman, Ghaith Nadir. Accidents can happen, but Nadir was an Iraqi refugee and asylum seeker—the very type of person Dutton had spent much of his political career vilifying and targeting with punitive policies and rhetoric. That alone gave the incident a clear subtext, but it was Dutton's response that turned a simple mishap into something more sinister.

Instead of showing concern or even mild embarrassment, Dutton shouted out that he "got him!," then made a joke about the cameraman not catching the ball, laughed it off, and suggested that had it been Albanese, he would have 'lied' about the whole incident. It was an oddly triumphant, almost gleeful reaction to an accident that left a man with a head injury—revealing a man more comfortable deflecting with ridicule than showing empathy. It was hard to shake the feeling that these moments weren't just gaffes—they had been brief insights into the leadership style on offer. Where empathy should have appeared, we saw sarcasm. Where humility might have made an impression, we saw bravado.

On the other side of the campaign trail, Albanese was confronted by a climate change protester, Alexa Stuart, furious about the government's continued approval of new coal and gas projects. She accused the Prime Minister of condemning her generation to a future of climate catastrophe, and she had every right to be angry: despite all the rhetoric about net zero and clean energy, Labor had green-lit 173 new fracking wells in Queensland and continued to approve existing fossil fuel projects under the fiction that they were not 'new' developments, but 'expansions'. But a bigger gas field is still a bigger gas field, and a deeper coal mine still burned more coal.

Albanese's response was to brush the incident off. He refused to comment, claiming that engaging would only encourage more protesters. But that was not a time to avoid engagement. Elections are one of the few moments when political pressure has real leverage—when leaders could be held to account by the very people they claimed to represent. Protest during a campaign wasn't a disruption; it was a democratic necessity. These weren't just votes at stake—they were lives, futures, and the shape of the planet to come. The climate crisis wasn't going to pause for polling day.

Those two incidents—one flippant, one furious—reflected deeper fractures in the political landscape. Dutton's football blunder became a metaphor for his political instinct to punch down and dismiss criticism with derision. Albanese's evasion of a powerful challenge from a young activist highlighted the contradiction between his party's climate narrative and its actions. But at the least, both moments had broken through the campaign veneer. And in a race already marked by strategic missteps and clichéd performances, it was those raw flashes of character that voters might have remembered most.

THE SILENCE OF THE BALLOT BOX: IGNORING GAZA

The killings in Gaza of fifteen medics and rescue workers by the Israel Defense Forces in early April had been one of the most horrifying international developments seen during a federal election campaign, in a spate of massacres that long crossed the boundaries of legality, morality, and humanity. All available evidence didn't suggest accidental crossfire or collateral damage, but targeted killings—executions in the service of a slow, methodical ethnic cleansing campaign by the state of Israel. It was a campaign which had claimed the lives of women, children, aid workers, journalists, and civilians of all types. The pretext, endlessly repeated by Israel and parroted by its international allies, was that Hamas was somehow responsible, but the nature of these victims—their roles, ages, and identities—told another completely different story. Medics are not militants. Babies are not insurgents. And yet, this indiscriminate slaughter continued, cheered on by the state of Israel and met with complicity, cowardice, and silence from much of the international community—including Australia.

In any democracy built on morality and the rule of law, a moment like that—when the world witnessed a slow genocide, broadcast in real time—should have provoked urgent political debate. But during Australia's federal election campaign, there had been a glaring absence. Labor did not talk about Gaza. The Coalition did not talk about Gaza—except to score points on anti-Semitism—and the mainstream media, with a few notable exceptions, hardly questioned them at all. It was as though the issue of Gaza—one that moved hundreds of thousands of Australians to protest, to grieve, and to question their own government's international allegiances—simply didn't exist within the official campaign narrative, as though the conflict had never happened and was an illusion.

Anthony Albanese was aware that any criticism of Israel could and would be quickly weaponised as an accusation of anti-Semitism—a smear that already crippled political debate in Britain, the United States, and many other countries in the Western world. Rather than confront this risk head-on, the Labor Party opted for evasion: relying on vague talking points, offering sterile platitudes, and hoping the issue didn't appear in the public view before election day. When Foreign Minister Penny Wong was asked about the killing of those fifteen medics, she responded not with outrage or condemnation, but with bureaucratic diplomacy. There needed to be a "full and thorough investigation," she said, and a need for protection of humanitarian workers under international law, suggesting that Australia was working with other countries on a "declaration" to that effect. A 'declaration' was all Australia could offer at the time? On parchment, or sent via e-mail? Or perhaps a post on Twitter? A declaration of cowardice—that was all it was.

This was the language of delay, of ambiguity, and of passive complicity. It wasn't designed to call out war crimes, or hold power to account, or provide moral clarity. It was designed to appease, and to downplay any public debate. Labor took refuge in the bland language of 'international humanitarian law,' knowing that these mechanisms were slow, ineffective, and easily bypassed by powerful vassal states such as Israel. A 'declaration' wouldn't stop bombs. A statement about the importance of 'every innocent life' wouldn't bring back the dead. And a generic call for a ceasefire, without demanding accountability from those committing the crimes, wasn't a political position—it was just an abdication of responsibility.

The Prime Minister, too, offered little of substance. Albanese acknowledged the trauma felt by Australians with families in Gaza, Israel, or Lebanon, but quickly moved back to cautious generalities. Every innocent life mattered, he said. Australia wanted a ceasefire and wanted hostages released. And then came the inevitable cliché of the 'two-state solution'—a phrase that nobody understood the meaning of anymore, and in the context of Israel's ongoing settlement expansion, military occupation, and *de facto* annexation, became little more than a diplomatic ghost. It was a slogan with no plan behind it, no timeline, no enforcement, and no credibility. And it was used because it allowed politicians to appear principled while doing nothing about the issue.

If the Labor government could not speak clearly about such an issue during an election campaign—and on an issue that was so clearly defined within the Labor Platform—if it could not defend the rights of journalists, doctors, and children not to be bombed into oblivion, then what did it stand for? How many more headless children did it need to see being held by grieving parents before it could go beyond the stage of offering meaningless platitudes and gratuitous declarations?

THE GREENS SPOKE UP ON GAZA

While the major parties buried their heads in the diplomatic sand, one political force in Australia consistently refused to look away. The Australian Greens emerged as the only parliamentary party willing to speak with moral clarity about what was happening in Gaza, and called it what it was: genocide. While Labor and the Coalition tiptoed around the truth, desperate to avoid offending powerful lobbyists or inviting bad-faith accusations of anti-Semitism, the Greens campaigned unapologetically on a platform grounded in international law, human rights, and humanitarian principles.

The leader of the Greens, Adam Bandt, didn't mince his words: "Tens of thousands of children have been killed," he said, "a health care system has been destroyed... people's homes have been reduced to rubble". Bandt also pointed out that this was not a radical opinion but a matter of public record, supported by reports from organisations such as Amnesty International and corroborated by the International Criminal Court, which issued arrest warrants for Israeli Prime Minister Benjamin Netanyahu. In an age where truth was filtered, managed, and spun into silence, the Greens opted for confrontation—willing to challenge the orthodoxy of Australia's outdated foreign policy influenced by Israel and the U.S., and risked a political backlash to stand on the side of justice.

This was not a fringe opinion. As the death toll in Gaza climbed and images of mass graves, bombed-out hospitals, and murdered medics circulated globally, more Australians began to demand that their government take a stand. But it was only the Greens—and a few independents in electorates with high Muslim populations—who were prepared to call out the obvious: a genocide was being perpetrated by Israel, and the Western world was watching on and aiding this genocide, including Australia.

While the Gaza issue didn't reshape the entire election outcome, it did influence thousands of votes. In tightly contested seats—such as those in inner Melbourne—those votes mattered. For many Australians, particularly younger and ethnically diverse voters who saw the situation with a sense of moral urgency, Labor's timidity was seen as a betrayal. These voters weren't confused by the talking points about 'balance' and 'both side-ism'—they saw a state with overwhelming military power crushing a besieged population—and a Western-backed government too cowardly to call it for what it was.

That cowardice was further exposed when comparing the Greens' straightforward language with Labor's evasive rhetoric. Where Senator Wong hid behind procedural jargon and vague diplomatic gestures, Bandt confronted the brutal reality of a military occupation, settler violence, and the long-standing refusal of Israel to recognise Palestinian sovereignty. He linked peace to justice; he tied any resolution to the fundamental requirement of ending the occupation. And most importantly, he pointed the finger at Australia's complicity: the military contracts, the diplomatic cover, the deference to Israeli lobby groups who shaped domestic narratives through fear and misinformation. Even the final atrocity during the campaign—where Israeli forces bombed clearly marked ambulances belonging to the Red Crescent—failed to stir outrage from the government. First, Israel lied: it claimed the vehicles weren't identifiable. Then, as footage emerged showing sirens blazing and markings visible in plain sight, the truth was undeniable. And yet again, silence from the Australian government: no condemnation; no consequences; no re-evaluation of diplomatic or military ties. Just the same mealy-mouthed statements about implementing more ceasefires that Israel didn't abide by, and platitudes about 'balanced positions'. The facts were there for all to see, but those in power preferred the politics of evasion.

THE BLOWBACK IN MULTICULTURAL AREAS

The Albanese government's silence and indifference on Gaza wasn't without electoral consequences. While there were certain seats in western Sydney that felt some of that heat—Watson and Blaxland—the more significant electoral blowback occurred in Melbourne, placing Labor under increasing strain in seats where multicultural identity, foreign policy, and local politics were strongly mixed. Two electorates in inner Melbourne—Wills and Macnamara—offered a clear test for whether Labor could hold together a fragile coalition of support amid an international crisis it refused to confront honestly.

Ultimately, none of these seats were lost by the Labor government at the election, although there where candidates supported by the Muslim Votes group who registered between 15 to 20 per cent of the primary vote. How much did Gaza affect these final results? Did it influence the outcomes in the seat of Melbourne, where Bandt ended up losing his seat, even though he was an outspoken advocate for Palestine? Voters were dealing with soaring rents, housing shortages, and climate change, and these were the bread-and-butter issues that every candidate had to address. But the genocide committed by Israel in Gaza hovered in the background—not as a distraction, but as a test of political and moral integrity, and not just in Melbourne or in western Sydney. It became a proxy for whether candidates truly represented the values of their constituents or just echoed the empty rhetoric of the Labor–Liberal foreign policy consensus.

Labor ended up in a difficult electoral position, but it was all of its own making. In trying to be all things to all people—offering strong support to the Jewish community and tepid words to Islamic communities, but avoiding hard truths—it alienated both. In one electorate, it lost trust for not being supportive enough of Israel; in another, for refusing to hold Israel to account. This double bind reflected the broader crisis of moral leadership that haunted the Albanese government's foreign policy posture. The party's refusal to confront the reality of Gaza, to speak with clarity and principle, eroded its moral standing, even if it didn't lose any seats because of this issue.

As preference flows and final rankings became decisive, the Gaza conflict left a mark on this election in ways few anticipated. Not with sweeping national swings, but through precise, community-driven acts of electoral defiance in places where silence felt like betrayal and inaction felt like complicity. The lesson for the Labor Party was clear: in an era where the personal is political and the global is local, foreign policy silence and trying to appease one group over another, may no longer be a safe political strategy.

A MASTERCLASS IN POLITICAL FAILURE

The third week of the federal election campaign had confirmed what many political observers had suspected a couple of weeks earlier: the Liberal Party's campaign was not just failing—it was falling apart. And while the previous week was best described as disastrous, the third week was arguably even worse. Where most governments benefited from incumbency by running disciplined, focused, and generally positive campaigns—touting achievements, pushing hopeful messaging, and strategically avoiding pitfalls—what had been seen from Peter Dutton and the Coalition was the opposite: a miserable, mistake-ridden, directionless, and relentlessly negative campaign that appeared to lack the energy or coherence required to inspire confidence with the electorate.

It wasn't just the gloom-laden dystopian talking points about Australia being on the brink of collapse—it was the absence of a compelling alternative vision. The Coalition had placed all its eggs in one basket: trying to convince the electorate that everything—*absolutely* everything—was so bad, and only getting worse, and that the Labor government was to blame for absolutely everything. Nothing was good... it was all so terrible.

Yet, as comprehensive as this message had been, it was a message that failed to have the impact that was intended. The supposed dystopia Dutton wanted Australians to believe in simply didn't reflect reality. The sun still rose, people still went about their lives, and while challenges existed—as they always did—Australians didn't appear to be buying into the apocalyptic narrative being peddled by the Coalition, if the opinion polls were to be believed. It was a strategy that felt increasingly out of touch with how most voters actually experienced the world.

At the centre of this malaise was Dutton himself—a leader whose performance had been characterised by mistakes and a lack of political groundwork, not just during the campaign, but for the entire parliamentary term. For someone who had had three years to prepare for the campaign, Dutton seemed astonishingly unready and underprepared. Compared to previous opposition leaders: Bill Shorten had used his six years to criss-cross the country, regularly subjecting himself to hostile town hall meetings, testing policy ideas, and building a campaign machine. Anthony Albanese, while less aggressive and productive during his time as leader of the opposition, had still made use of every available moment in opposition to refine his messaging and build credibility.

Dutton, on the other hand, had spent the bulk of his time in the right-wing media bubble—appearing regularly on Sky News and 2GB, ignoring critical outlets such as SBS, denouncing the ABC, and speaking only to a narrow audience already predisposed to support him. This wasn't a winning strategy for an opposition leader; it was a regression and the wiser heads within the Liberal Party—if any still existed—should have worked on broadening

Dutton's experience far earlier. Leadership demands visibility, flexibility, and effort. But Dutton frequently disappeared from public view when the going got tough. He failed to test ideas in the public arena, avoided uncomfortable questions, and relied instead on ideological comfort zones filled with culture war rhetoric and attacks on 'woke' media and 'indoctrinating' school education across Australia. This hadn't sharpened his message, it had done the opposite: it had dulled his appeal. It had left him unchallenged, untested, and unprepared for the rigours of a national election campaign. What emerged then was the result of that neglect: a leader lost in the fog of his own negativity, unable to present himself as a credible alternative Prime Minister. Why had nobody within his team prepared Dutton for this election campaign? Why had nobody noticed the clearly ringing alarm bells?

And what would a Dutton government even have looked like? At best, it would have been a Morrison government redux—without even the modest veneer of competence, considering the Morrison government had left behind a legacy of dysfunction, secrecy, and poor administration. The idea that voters were crying out for a return to that style of governance that they had clearly rejected at the 2022 federal election was delusional. For all the Coalition's attempts to stoke fear and division, the one thing it had failed to provide was a coherent sense of purpose—the *raison d'être* behind their bid for power. Once any of Dutton's campaign rhetoric was peeled back, there was no reason in the bid: it appeared to be power for the sake of power.

This was what made that campaign not just ineffective, but potentially one of the worst opposition efforts in recent memory.

There was no grand contest of ideas, no bold vision to debate, no clear sense of what the Liberal Party actually stood for beyond *not* being Labor, endlessly criticising the government, and wanting to be the government. Even those who might have been sympathetic to conservative principles were left cold by a campaign that seemed designed more to inflame than to inspire. And as pre-poll voting opened that week, time was rapidly running out to turn things around.

Australians wanted a government that functioned and worked for them—not one that just constantly offered blame. They wanted leadership—not constant complaints about the media or dog-whistling about woke culture. We had been there before—through Scott Morrison—and it seemed that the Liberal Party had picked up all the wrong lessons from the 2022 federal election result, which they had comprehensively lost. And while the Labor Party hadn't promised any type of revolutionary reform or provided anything outstanding to the electorate, at least it had offered a coherent and largely positive agenda. For the Liberals, the campaign had devolved into an excellent case study about what happened when an opposition failed to do the hard work, refused to grow beyond its ideological comfort zone, and underestimated the intelligence and optimism of the electorate.

THE WORST OPPOSITION CAMPAIGN IN POLITICAL HISTORY?

It was a question that kept coming up—among journalists, political analysts, and increasingly from the public itself: was this the worst election campaign run by an opposition in modern Australian political history? As the third week of the

2025 campaign drew to a close, it became increasingly clear that the Liberal Party's performance under Dutton was not just uninspiring—it was historically bad. And while the final judgment had to wait until election day, the signs already suggested that we had witnessed a campaign that would become the new benchmark for political failure.

To fairly assess whether it was the worst, it helps to reflect on past campaigns that had gone off the rails. The 2004 Labor campaign under Mark Latham was often cited as one of the most disastrous in living memory—not because it started poorly, but because it collapsed spectacularly in the final week with the announcement of a poorly conceived forestry package in Tasmania, and general perceptions about whether Latham was suitable or ready to become prime minister.

What had been shaping up as a competitive challenge to John Howard ended in humiliation, delivering Labor its worst two-party preferred result since the Great Depression era of 1931. Then there was John Hewson's 1993 campaign—the infamous 'birthday cake' GST interview that blew up what had been a well-structured campaign until that moment. Hewson's honesty in attempting to explain the complexities of his tax policy became the very issue that sank him, crystallising voter anxiety and ridicule in a single media moment.

But in each of these cases, the narrative of collapse hinged on a single major failure—Latham's handshake gaffe, poor forestry policy and erratic late-stage behaviour; Hewson's GST stumble, or even H.V. Evatt's paranoid mismanagement of the Petrov Affair in the 1954 campaign. What set the 2025 Liberal campaign apart was not one major blunder—it was the sheer, consistent and relentless accumulation of smaller ones. It started badly, it worsened each week, and there had been no sign of course correction. It was a campaign which seemed devoid of strategy, vision, or momentum, led by a figure who appeared more comfortable delivering apocalyptic soundbites than facing the public with credible policies.

Even among Liberal Party campaigns that were deemed poor, some had gone on to succeed due to external factors. Tony Abbott's 2010 campaign was scattergun and gaffe-prone, but still nearly toppled a first-term Labor government. Malcolm Turnbull's 2016 campaign was widely criticised for its lack of energy and clarity but ended in a narrow victory.

Scott Morrison's 2019 campaign was less a masterclass in politics than a masterclass in luck, bolstered by Labor's internal missteps and relentless support from News Corporation. What each of these examples shared was a degree of chaos—but also a broader media narrative and party apparatus and insiders working overtime to cover for that chaos. Dutton, in contrast, had run a campaign without cohesion or external cheerleaders. Even the Murdoch press, usually a reliable megaphone for the Coalition, had been lukewarm in its support: there hadn't been any *Australia Needs Peter* headlines (as there were for Tony Abbott in 2013); he wasn't being depicted as the 'man who saves Australia', or that Dutton was 'the answer'.

Dutton also carried baggage that previous Liberal leaders didn't. Persistent rumours about his past behaviours in the police force, his property wealth, and his temperament followed him into the campaign, even if they had never been substantiated in a way that could stick in a courtroom. But in the court of public opinion, perception always trumped reality. For a political figure to be continually haunted by questions about character—and to never properly address them—was a fatal flaw in any campaign, especially one that hinged so heavily on personal leadership credentials. It was too late in the campaign to have a "real Peter" moment, to replicate the attempts by Julia Gillard with her own *real Julia* moment which she had used to resurrect her faltering election campaign in 2010 and, aside from this, the electorate was seeing the real Peter anyway. There was no other persona or vaudeville act that he could switch to: *this was it*.

And then there was the issue of political vision. Whatever faults previous opposition campaigns may have had, most at least attempted to present a vision of what government under their leadership might look like. Latham had pushed a radical education agenda and a forestry policy that had merit but was poorly conceived; Hewson had economic reform; Evatt had the promise of postwar nation-building (however bungled in the delivery). Dutton's campaign, by contrast, offered little beyond fear and resentment.

Aside from nuclear energy—which was a half-baked proposal anyway—if there was a policy centrepiece, it was nowhere to be found. If there was an optimistic case for change, it hadn't been made. The campaign was driven almost entirely by slogans about restoring law and order and fighting 'wokeness'—hardly a compelling electoral message for the millions of Australians focused on housing affordability, wages, climate change, and cost-of-living pressures.

MOMENTUM MATTERS

As the election campaign headed into its final fortnight, one word began to appear more often: *momentum*. It was the intangible force that could carry a party to unexpected victory—or accelerate its descent into disaster. For the Coalition under Dutton, that force simply wasn't there; the opinion polls had slipped away when they needed to be flowing in their favour. After three chaotic and lacklustre weeks, there was no real sense that the Liberal Party had any forward motion at all. And while the Labor Party's campaign hadn't exactly electrified the electorate, it had presented itself as steady, competent, disciplined—and—most importantly, in the context of its previous time in office between 2010–13—not self-destructive.

Momentum in election campaigns is a curious thing: it was possible to have it and still lose. Labor had had it in both 2016 and 2019, where Bill Shorten's campaign in 2016 had closed the gap significantly and given Malcolm Turnbull a massive fright, and the 2019 campaign had generated genuine optimism and an expected victory among progressives—until it had all fallen apart on the day of the election. But the presence of momentum in both cases had signalled a party with energy, belief, and a message that at least part of the electorate had found compelling. By contrast, a campaign without momentum—especially one mired in negativity and confusion—had never succeeded in winning office, at least not in modern Australian political history.

Anthony Albanese had had this momentum in 2022: there had been a mood for change in the electorate and he had used it to move past a shaky start and lead the Labor Party to a modest but decisive victory. And while the 2025 Labor campaign wasn't bursting with innovation or bold policy reforms, it didn't need to be: it just needed to avoid major mistakes and let the Coalition implode under the weight of its own contradictions.

That wasn't to say it had been a landslide in the making. The 2025 election took place in a new political era—one where minor parties and independents had consolidated their place in the national political scene. Over a third of the electorate had voted outside the traditional two-party structure, and while that made the national vote share more unpredictable, it also supported the strong belief that the Coalition could not regain government without significant inroads into seats it had lost in recent elections—many of them lost to independents who were elected precisely because of a rejection of Liberal values and behaviour.

While the Liberal and National Coalition had been leading in the opinion polls before the election campaign commenced, many observers still believed it was virtually impossible for the Liberal Party to win a majority in its own right. A pathway to minority government also appeared to have been closed off. Too many of the electorates the party would have needed to flip were held by popular independents or were urban progressive seats where the Liberal brand had been damaged—perhaps beyond repair, unless major internal reforms were made. The party hadn't done the work to rebuild relationships with these communities, let alone articulate why it deserved to govern again.

Of course, in politics, nothing is impossible. A major scandal involving a senior Labor figure in the final weeks of the campaign could have changed the dynamics, but there had been no indication that such a scandal was looming. The best the opposition dirt units had managed were feeble attempts at character assassination—reheated rumours, personal attacks, or strange claims such as Anthony Albanese's failure to publicly kiss and acknowledge Tanya Plibersek at the Labor campaign launch as a sign of leadership instability. It was hardly *Watergate*. If the Coalition had been banking on an Albanese disaster to rescue their campaign, they weren't only clutching at straws—they were showing just how little agency they had left in the race.

It was also worth revisiting that old political adage: oppositions don't win elections, governments lose them. And while the Albanese government hadn't dazzled during the campaign, it hadn't self-sabotaged either. There had been no strong evidence suggesting the public had an insatiable appetite for change, as they did in 2013 and again in 2022. And even if there had been, Dutton hadn't offered any great reasons for the electorate to make a switch over to the Liberal Party.

And that was the deeper problem for the Coalition. They had failed to generate a momentum for change, and a campaign without momentum became a campaign of desperation: errors were made, and it bred paranoia, stunts, contradictions, and a disassociation from what was really happening in the campaign. That was what we had seen over the course of the first three campaign weeks. And while the final two weeks had still provided room for surprises, it wasn't enough time to reverse the trajectory of a campaign that had been broken from the start.

So, who had the momentum? At that point, Labor had been moving forward in all the right ways. The Coalition, meanwhile, staggered towards the finish line, weighed down by its own inertia. Of course, events can always change things, and the unexpected can always arrive quickly from the horizon, when it was least expected.

And leaders could, all of a sudden, change tack. But Dutton didn't appear to be the crazy–brave maverick who could throw caution to the wind and exploit the new circumstances that might have appeared after a disruption. He simply wasn't that sort of leader. Unless something extraordinary happened, the final fortnight of the campaign was always going to confirm what the campaign had already revealed: Dutton's Liberal–National Party was out of time, out of touch, out of ideas, and out of momentum.

THE FICTION OF FIXING AUSTRALIA'S HOUSING CRISIS

As the 2025 federal election campaign entered its final stages, housing became the headline issue—and for many good reasons. In most parts of Australia, housing affordability was at crisis levels, home ownership was slipping out of reach for an entire generation, and homelessness was on the rise. With the two major parties locked in a battle over who could present the more convincing solution, voters were bombarded with promises that, on the surface, sounded bold and decisive—but were little more than hollow gestures likely to exacerbate the very problems they claimed to address.

The Labor Party launched its housing pitch in the final week of the campaign with fanfare, led by Prime Minister Anthony Albanese and Housing Minister Clare O'Neil. "More homes and smaller deposits" was Albanese's main pitch, coupled with a vague assurance that "this isn't theoretical—this is happening". O'Neil promised renters a better deal and first-home buyers a smoother path into the market, while emphasising Labor's plans would improve housing supply.

Meanwhile, opposition leader Peter Dutton—not to be outdone—announced a policy designed to "drive up home ownership" by making loan repayments tax deductible, increasing supply and cutting demand through a reduction in Australia's migration intake—even though it wasn't clear how the 'driving up' part would actually be achieved. "That's what we're on about here, drive up home ownership," he said, repeating the same phrase with the same emphasis as though saying it twice might make it more coherent and memorable.

But behind the political theatre there was a reality that was being ignored—economists across the board criticised the plans from both parties as economically illiterate and strategically misleading. Despite their superficial differences, the policies from both camps shared a common flaw: they failed to confront the structural causes of Australia's housing crisis, and in some cases, would make them even worse.

For decades, Australia's housing market had been distorted by a series of short-term fixes and politically expedient incentives that ignored the long-term consequences. The First Home Owners Grant, introduced by the Howard government in 2000 with a $7,000 sweetener to help buyers overcome stamp duty costs and the implementation of the GST at the time, was a classic example. Predictably, house prices rose by roughly the same amount, cancelling out any real benefit to buyers and, instead, inflated the market. Those who could already afford a home received the benefits; those just outside the threshold were left further behind. The policy, well-intentioned as it might have been—and that stretched credibility and the benefit of doubt as far as possible—misunderstood how markets respond to demand-side subsidies without an equal or greater increase in supply.

During the 2025 election campaign, the same flawed logic was repeated, as it had been over the past twenty-five years in federal and state politics. Offering financial incentives to buyers—whether through lower deposits or targeted grants—without addressing land availability, construction rates, zoning restrictions, and rental security, just added fuel to the already massive housing bonfire. Demand increased, prices rose, and affordability declined even further. Real estate agents might have been very happy about these outcomes, but for ordinary Australians, they remained an ongoing disaster.

Neither party appeared ready to challenge the most sacred cows of the housing policy debate—and the most obvious: negative gearing and capital gains tax concessions for investors. These mechanisms turned housing from a basic human need into a financial investment asset, distorting incentives across the board. Investors were rewarded for snapping up multiple properties, pushing up prices and rents, and competing directly with aspiring homeowners. As long as these tax arrangements remained untouched, boosting the supply-side alone would not change anything—especially when many of the new homes being built were aimed not at low- or middle-income earners, but at the upper end of the market or the speculative investor class.

The housing crisis was not just an issue about economics, but of values. What is housing for? Is it a commodity for accumulating wealth, or a public good that ensures shelter for everyone? If the objective was to get roofs over heads, the solution was straightforward: build more public housing, in urban centres and regional towns. Abandon the failed experiment of privatised solutions and instead fund, manage and maintain government-owned dwellings designed for long-term use, not short-term profit. Certainly, the federal government committed to building more housing through the Housing Australia Future Fund, but it was just a drop in the ocean: 40,000 additional dwellings over five years—or an average of three houses in each suburb across Australia—was simply not enough.

The policy alternatives existed—but the political appetite to offer something different was just not there. And in an election campaign where housing headlines won the votes, both Labor and the Liberals seemed more interested in appearing to do something, rather than actually solving the problem itself: it was a competition of nothingness. These policies were carefully crafted illusions—gestures aimed at pacifying public frustration without threatening the structural drivers of the crisis. And for as long as that continued, housing in Australia remained a privilege for the wealthy and the already-there propertied class, and not a right for the many.

HOW NEOLIBERALISM HIJACKED AUSTRALIA'S HOUSING MARKET

To understand why housing in Australia reached a crisis point in 2025, it's important to look beyond the soundbites of the federal election campaign and examine how we got here. This housing crisis wasn't created through some natural disaster or calamitous economic collapse—it was the result of decades of political choices rooted in neoliberal ideology and a systemic redefinition of housing from a basic human necessity into a wealth-generating asset class.

The roots for this went back to the early 1980s with the rise of Thatcherism in the United Kingdom. Margaret Thatcher's

'Right to Buy' policy encouraged public housing tenants to purchase their homes at a discount, reducing the stock of social housing while forcing through a new Hayekian economic and cultural model: private home ownership not just as a right, but as a moral virtue. This ideological shift then appeared in other parts of the world, including Australia, where successive governments of all persuasions embraced home ownership as a tool for individual wealth creation and political loyalty.

In Australia, this ideological shift crystallised during the Howard era. In 2000, the Howard government halved the capital gains tax on assets held for more than a year and retained the ability for property investors to negatively gear—meaning they could deduct losses on rental properties from their taxable income. The combination of these two changes made property speculation vastly more attractive, incentivising Australians to invest in their second, third, or even tenth home, and turning ordinary middle-class households into miniature investment firms.

By 2023, over 2.2 million Australians owned investment properties, and 71 per cent of all new property loans went to investors, not first-home buyers. More than 20 per cent of landlords owned multiple investment properties, with some holding portfolios of five or more dwellings. In the same period, only about 30 per cent of new housing stock was accessible to first-time buyers. Meanwhile, public housing stock declined from 6 per cent of total housing in the early 1990s to less than 3 per cent, according to the Australian Institute of Health and Welfare. The remaining public housing was concentrated in disadvantaged areas, underfunded, and stigmatised—a major change from its original role as a core pillar of social stability.

This transformation of housing into a speculative asset—one protected and inflated by tax policy—fuelled a self-perpetuating cycle of unaffordability. Every election brought a new round of incentives designed to appear helpful, even if they were not: first-home buyer grants, deposit schemes, shared equity models. But these demand-side policies only served to increase purchasing power without expanding supply, pushing prices up further and worsening inequality.

The root problem was not just a shortage of houses: it was the systemic design of a housing economy that favoured capital appreciation over shelter. It was the belief that property was a market first and a home second. It was the deliberate political cowardice that refused to make changes to negative gearing or capital gains tax discounts—despite clear economic evidence that these policies distorted the market and forced prices up.

The COVID-19 pandemic added complexity to an already volatile system. Population growth paused, construction slowed due to supply chain disruptions and labour shortages, and investors with financial buffers held on while prices continued to rise. But the post-pandemic recovery saw a rapid resurgence in population movement and migration, particularly to regional areas and outer suburbs—just as interest rates rose and inflation eroded real wages. Renters, particularly low-income earners, were severely impacted. In 2024, rents in Sydney and Melbourne rose by over 30 per cent, with regional areas such as Ballarat, Sunshine Coast, and Launceston not far behind. Vacancy rates in some cities fell below 1 per cent, triggering bidding wars for basic accommodation.

This broken system did not serve tenants or aspiring homeowners: it benefited those who already owned multiple properties, enjoyed tax subsidies, and sat on appreciating assets while the rest of the population struggled with unaffordable rents and impossible entry points into the housing market.

Solutions do exist—but they require courage and a willingness to rethink the role of housing in Australian society. One option is to reintroduce public housing at far greater scale—just as governments did in the post-war period in the 1950s and 1960s—not just for the most vulnerable, but as a viable, long-term alternative to private renting or ownership. This could have taken the form of mixed-income developments, integrated into existing communities, professionally managed, and well-designed.

Secondly, Australia needs to confront its tax policy distortions head-on. Negative gearing should have been phased out or restricted to new builds, while capital gains tax discounts should have been wound back, particularly for short-term speculative sales. This would not only have curbed demand from investors, but also begun to restore fairness to a system that heavily favoured wealth over work.

Third, tenancy law reform is essential. The fear that stronger tenant rights would destroy the investment market is misplaced—in reality, long-term tenants who treat homes with care are a better prospect than frequent turnover, rent arrears, and vacancy losses. Germany's housing system, which emphasises stable long-term renting and discourages speculation, offers a different model that is worth studying.

Short-term rental platforms such as Airbnb and Stayz need to be regulated. Entire homes listed as perpetual short stays reduces long-term supply, inflates local housing markets, and hollows out neighbourhoods. Cities such as Amsterdam, Berlin and Barcelona have introduced caps, taxation, or outright bans on such practices, and Australia should follow suit before tourist pressure further cannibalises the rental stock.

The housing crisis in Australia is not just a matter of economics—it's a symptom of a deeper social and political failure. It reflects the dominance of neoliberal thinking, where everything is commodified, even the roof over one's head. Until we reclaim housing as a public good, treat it as infrastructure, and design policies that serve people rather than profits, the crisis is destined to continue—no matter which party is in power or how many new grants they offer in the lead-up to election day.

THE LONG ROAD BACK: RECLAIMING THE SOUL OF HOUSING

If Australia was ever to overcome this housing crisis, it would take more than policy tweaks and political promises—it would require a deep and deliberate shift in mindset. The psychology of home ownership in this country had been fundamentally transformed over the past twenty-five years, where a home is less likely to be viewed as a place to live, raise a family, and contribute to a community. Instead, it is an investment vehicle, a tool for wealth accumulation, a line item in a portfolio. To address the crisis in any meaningful way, this commodified view of housing needs to be reimagined—and that process could take a generation.

By 2025, this mindset on property as an investment was embedded not only in the financial system but in the culture itself. Home ownership was presented as the pinnacle of financial success—there isn't anything inherently wrong with owning or wanting to own a home, but it's not the only way to live or contribute to the world. Those without property ownership are seen as transient, unstable, or financially imprudent—or *just renting*—despite working full-time jobs, paying exorbitant rents, and often being better budgeters than those who hold multiple properties. Young people are encouraged to 'get into the market' as early as possible, as though they were investing in stocks, not securing a basic human need.

But reversing this deeply ingrained psychology isn't going to be quick. Just as it took twenty-five years to arrive at this distorted reality, it could take another twenty-five years to undo it—and that's assuming that the process began now, which it clearly hadn't. Every year the issue is kicked further down the road; every election brings in new demand-side incentives that reinforce the housing-as-commodity type of thinking.

Every parliamentary debate on housing reform is clouded by the personal interests of MPs and senators who own multiple investment properties. As of 2024, nearly half of federal parliamentarians owned at least one investment property, a clear conflict of interest that undermined any attempt at genuine reform.

This concentration of property ownership among lawmakers and political donors has created a structural bias in favour of the status quo. Who among them would willingly legislate themselves into a lower net worth? And yet that is exactly what true reform requires: measures that reduce speculative investment, lower housing returns, and reset the housing economy in favour of a liveable future, not profit.

This is not to say people shouldn't be able to build wealth or plan for their futures—but we need to ask at what cost. When the housing aspirations and simple living of millions are diminished to maintain the capital gains of a few, Australia can no longer be considered a fair society. A home has to be seen first as shelter, then as security, and only then—if at all—as an asset.

Changing how a society thinks about housing is never going to be easy—but the country has to start somewhere. It requires political courage, sustained advocacy, and new forms of narratives about housing and living as a citizen in a community. The sooner we begin, the sooner we can reach the future that we all claim we want to have: an Australia where a home is something you live in, not something you hoarded.

A STRANGE, DISJOINTED WEEK IN THE CAMPAIGN END GAME

The fourth week of the federal election campaign in late April has a different feel to it—a strange, fragmented few full days and a disjointed rhythm. With Easter Monday and ANZAC Day having started and ended the week, there were just three formal campaigning days in between, and these were overshadowed by the major global event of the death of Pope Francis. While almost 40 per cent of Australians have no religious affiliation and only 20 per cent identify as Catholic, the Pope was an international figure of stature, and his death subdued the campaign atmosphere, making an already difficult task for Peter Dutton even more difficult. Campaigning lost its energy, major events were paused, and both Anthony Albanese and Dutton suspended their activities to attend church—a truce in an otherwise relentless campaign.

Early pre-poll voting had begun on the Tuesday of week four, which signified a major change in the campaign—the election was no longer a theoretical exercise; no longer just about changing minds; the election was suddenly *very real* with *real votes* being lodged. A record 542,000 Australians cast their votes on the first day of pre-polling, with around two million by the end of the week—meaning that by election day on May 3, close to half the electorate had already voted. This change in recent times from an *election day* to an *election period*—voting stretched across two weeks—made it more difficult for all candidates to sustain momentum, but it did reward discipline, consistency and energy.

This had always been a Coalition campaign running against the tide—a challenger needs a clean path to build momentum: a routine, a rhythm, a clear run of days to hammer home messages and shift voter sentiment. Instead, the Coalition had to deal with a messy timetable—school holidays, two long weekends, public holidays, and then the death of a global religious leader. A campaign that had already stumbled through its first three weeks was thrown further into disarray just at a time when it needed to be coherent.

Of course, such a disjointed timetable also impacted the Labor Party, but as the incumbent and the frontrunners, they didn't need to build a momentum for change: Albanese didn't need to convince an electorate of change—he just had to reassure them that *stability* was preferable to *risk*. And while dissatisfaction with Labor had been simmering, there didn't seem to be a 'change the government' mood in the air. In contrast, Dutton faced mounting problems not just with voters, but within his own party: leaks continued to flow directly to Labor strategists, bypassing the media entirely.

In a campaign week where building momentum was absolutely critical, the Coalition found itself stranded by events outside its control and by its own ineptitude. The question was not whether Dutton could pull off a miracle comeback in the final weeks—it had been about how the Liberal Party could lessen the expected loss, and whether they could avoid an even more catastrophic result than expected.

THE COALITION CAMPAIGNS ON DEFENCE, BUT THE MESSAGE MISFIRES

As the Coalition struggled to find footing during the week, it turned to what it believed was one of its few remaining strengths: defence policy. In Perth, Peter Dutton and shadow defence minister Andrew Hastie announced a $21 billion boost to defence spending, framing it as essential to Australia's national security and regional stability, and that the "single most important task for the Australian government is to keep the Australian people safe," positioning this as an imperative for maintaining alliances and deterring threats.

Yet while playing to perceived strengths was a textbook campaigning tactic, the Coalition's defence pitch exposed further problems within its election strategy. The announcement lacked depth, offering little detail beyond big-ticket spending figures and a parade of militaristic slogans. There was no discussion about veterans' services, no proposals for reforming the Australian Defence Force's outdated structures, and no vision for modernising the force to meet the complex, non-traditional threats of the twenty-first century. Missing too was any reflection on Australia's strained regional relationships—and how careless diplomacy under Dutton's previous time in office as defence minister, including recent inflammatory remarks about Indonesia and Russia, had jeopardised Australia's standing in the region.

Even more baffling was how Dutton proposed to fund this $21 billion spend: reversing Labor's HECS debt reduction policy, scrapping subsidies for electric vehicles, and reversing tax cuts promised by the Labor government—hardly a recipe for electoral success. Few voters, irrespective of income bracket, wanted to surrender tax relief for the promise of more F-35 fighter jets or military hardware, particularly when trust in defence procurement had been low after years of scandals, blowouts, and wastage.

Dutton then went down yet another culture war cul-de-sac, pushing for anti-Semitism questions to be added to the Australian citizenship test and suggesting a new round of scrutiny of existing Palestinian visa approvals. These were naked appeals to the Zionist lobby and attempts to wedge Labor on national security, but again, they felt out of step with the current priorities of the electorate: cost-of-living pressures, health, housing, and education dominated voter concerns—not heavy-handed changes to citizenship tests or ethno-political dog-whistling.

It was true that the Liberal Party historically polled better on defence, economic management, and border security but as the years had rolled on, that reputation had become frayed. The myth of Coalition superiority on economic management crumbled in the face of Labor's record in office: the evidence suggested that the Liberal Party was not the better economic manager, yet the perception persisted. On border security and immigration, Dutton's heavy-handedness alienated moderate voters and reinforced an image of cruelty over competence.

Defence remained as the last symbolic refuge—but even there, the Coalition's approach was intellectually thin and politically tone-deaf. It focused on spending billions with no accompanying narrative about how Australia could genuinely strengthen itself without alarming neighbours such as Indonesia or inflaming tensions in a volatile world.

Instead, Dutton's defence policy felt trapped in a twentieth-century mindset—obsessed with the boys' toys and geopolitical sabre-rattling—while Australia's real needs in the Indo–Pacific area demanded a far more thoughtful, deft, and forward-looking approach. Hastie's military background might have lent credibility to these announcements, but experience in combat does not necessarily translate into strategic wisdom in procurement, diplomacy, or military reform.

Ultimately, this defence announcement revealed more about the Coalition's weaknesses than its strengths. It highlighted a party unable to adapt to modern campaigning realities, unable to read the room, and increasingly speaking to a shrinking, aging base that wanted to hear that everything could be solved by spending on fighter jets and tightening immigration controls: it felt less like a bold and enticing move and more like a desperate one.

MORE LEADERS' DEBATES, BUT WHERE'S THE INSPIRATION?

The fourth week also had two debates—Nine/Fairfax's *The Great Debate* and Seven West's *The Final Showdown*—and both delivered what was to be expected: tightly controlled, stage-managed events that offered more of the same arguments in slightly different packaging. In these more direct formats, both Albanese and Dutton faced a series of timed questions from political commentators and moderators, and were forced to answer within a strict window of sixty seconds. These tighter formats did inject some energy, but the substance remained predictable, and the debates quickly descended into the same familiar campaign themes.

Perhaps the most revealing moment of *The Great Debate* came not from the leaders but from moderator Ally Langdon—a theme also picked up by *The Final Showdown*—who asked why neither leader was inspiring the public. Neither Albanese nor Dutton could convincingly answer it, because both major parties—and the media structures that covered them—had long abandoned the idea of truly inspirational politics. In Australia, political courage was punished, not rewarded; big, community-centred ideas were demolished by corporate media before they could ever take hold.

What would 'inspirational' leadership even look like? Not another round of tax cuts for the wealthy or shallow slogans about choice and opportunity, but bold systemic changes: super-profits taxes on mining giants such as Gina Rinehart or Andrew Forrest, free higher education and dental care, massive investment in public housing, demilitarising Australia's foreign policy, rebuilding a genuine sense of national community. But such policies are anathema to the neoliberal orthodoxy that both major parties largely accept and the mainstream media vigorously promotes. Instead of collective inspiration, politics focuses almost entirely on individual aspiration, ignoring the social contract in favour of a perpetual rat race and a fear of missing out.

A STRANGE, DISJOINTED WEEK IN THE CAMPAIGN END GAME

This was the tragedy underlying Australian democracy: a political culture so dominated by market dogma and corporate media interests that even modest reforms are treated as radical, and the language of collective responsibility becomes increasingly absent from the national conversation. Political debates, as a result, become risk-averse exercises in messaging discipline, not moments of inspiration: leaders don't inspire anymore because they weren't trained to do so.

It wasn't that individual ambition and entrepreneurialism has no place—they do, and can flourish within a broader social framework. But without public investment, functioning health and education systems, decent infrastructure, and a vibrant middle class, individual success stories were nothing but shallow myths. Even billionaires owed their fortunes to collective efforts—roads, education systems, stable governments and other people—which they rarely acknowledged until their fortunes were at risk and they pleaded for bailouts.

These two debates, while marginally sharper than the previous two, ultimately changed little. Albanese reiterated his focus on health, Medicare, education, and the promise that "no one will be held back and no one left behind," a refrain from his 2022 campaign. Dutton stuck to crime, law and order, and defence—ground he retreated to repeatedly throughout the campaign. The media in *The Great Debate* declared Dutton the winner by a margin of two votes to one—the studio jury in *The Final Showdown* was far more comprehensive for Albanese, registering 50 per cent in favour, to Dutton's 25 per cent—but winning or losing a debate in the dying weeks of a campaign meant little when much of the electorate had already voted, or made up their minds long ago.

And in truth, winning those debates had little bearing on winning elections. History was littered with leaders who dominated debates but lost at the ballot box: Kevin Rudd against Tony Abbott in 2013, Julia Gillard against Abbott in 2010 (that resulted in a minority government), Bill Shorten against Scott Morrison in 2019. These sterile, tightly managed performances didn't sway elections—they just provided momentary grist for media spin cycles and a few viral clips for social media.

THE OPINION POLLS CONTINUED TO PROVIDE BAD NEWS FOR THE COALITION

A new round of opinion polls released that week crystallised what had been obvious for some time: the Labor government was pulling ahead, and the Coalition was falling further behind. The Morgan poll showed the most dramatic movement, giving Labor a commanding 55.5 per cent to 44.5 per cent two-party-preferred lead over the Coalition—a gap that, historically, no opposition had ever managed to overturn in the final week of a campaign. YouGov and Newspoll results showed similar patterns, indicating not just a drift towards Labor, but a hardening of voter sentiment as pre-poll voting continued.

Comparisons with the 2022 election showed that at the same stage in the campaign, the numbers had been almost identical. Although opinion polls could never guarantee the final result—as the 2019 election proved—the dynamics in 2025 were even more daunting for the Liberal Party. Unlike 2019, where voters harboured deep doubts about the leadership of Bill Shorten, there was no clear rejection of Albanese. And unlike Scott Morrison's last-minute surge in 2019, Dutton had no pool of goodwill to draw upon: there was just not much there. His belated attempts at softening his image had come too late and too inconsistently to have any real impact.

It is often said during election campaigns that "it's never over until it's over," but even seasoned political observers were scraping the bottom of the barrel trying to imagine a scenario where Dutton could pull off a reversal. Even traditionally hostile media outlets such as Sky News struggled to put a positive spin on Dutton's performance, with some conservative commentators openly acknowledging the Liberal campaign had been a disaster.

Dutton missed the opportunity not just to win government, but to position the Liberal Party credibly for the next election. Throughout the campaign, Dutton oscillated between two personas: the aggressive ex-cop who seemed constantly one question away from snapping, and the awkward, softer image briefly glimpsed during the debate after the death of Pope Francis. But even when Dutton tried to project calmness, it felt strained, temporary, and at odds with his broader political identity. The day after the debate, he reverted to form—aggressive, combative, defensive, and belligerent when challenged by journalists.

This inability to consistently reframe his public persona was a major failing, especially when it had been obvious for years that the 'hard man' image was almost impossible to sell to a broader Australian electorate. Dutton had nearly three years to soften his edges, to offer a new, more constructive vision. Instead, he remained trapped by his past, and by a party apparatus either unwilling or unable to modernise itself.

A SYSTEM IN DESPERATE NEED OF RENEWAL

As the federal election campaign entered its final week, the overall picture became clearer: a more energised although cautious Labor government seemed to be veering towards re-election, and a disjointed and disorganised Coalition struggled to remain relevant. It had been a lugubrious and turgid campaign in many ways, defined more by what was left unsaid than by bold promises or visionary ideas. Yet within that, the broader currents of Australian politics were exposed—a deep aversion to risk, a media and political system reluctant to engage with real change, and a widening disconnect between the political class and the communities they were meant to serve.

The issues that had been ignored during the campaign—Indigenous justice, climate change, poverty, homelessness, gambling reform, structural inequality—weren't going to just vanish after the election. These issues would keep growing and will eventually demand political attention, whether leaders during that term were prepared for it or not, and whether they liked it or not. The campaign had been a missed opportunity to address these issues; to lay the foundations for a renewed, fairer Australia. Instead, the political establishment offered a holding pattern, a rearguard action against change rather than a bold leap towards it.

An electorate that may have reluctantly endorsed stability and re-elected the Labor government this time around would, over the coming years, demand more: more ambition, more action, more courage. If Albanese's government failed to deliver it, a new generation of independents, minor parties, and community movements would rise to fill the void.

A STRANGE, DISJOINTED WEEK IN THE CAMPAIGN END GAME

Australian politics was changing—slowly, unevenly, but inevitably: the old party duopoly was weakening. The demands for structural reform, democratic renewal, and genuine social progress were growing louder. The 2025 election might not have been the evolution many had hoped for, but it may have provided another small step towards a different political future—one where inspiration was not a dirty word, and where government was about building something bigger than the sum of its political calculations.

HOW COST OF LIVING FEAR WAS SHAPED FOR POLITICAL GAIN

It was clear throughout most of the campaign, that it was being framed as the 'cost of living election'. In fact, for most of the parliamentary term, the media drove a continuous and sustained narrative that living costs were spiralling out of control, ever since the Labor government took office in May 2022—even though inflation and price rises began during the final year of the Coalition government. This was always a difficult area to debate, because once it was pointed out that things were not quite as catastrophic as the media portrayed, these people were instantly labelled as out of touch, privileged snobs, or totally oblivious to the struggles of ordinary families.

There was no question that prices, rents, and mortgage repayments increased over the past three years, but this trend was already underway well before Labor's term commenced. What was often overlooked was that the real underlying issue was not simply rising prices—it was the widening gap between the rich and the poor, a reality that neither the Labor Party nor the Coalition seriously addressed. Instead, the political focus during that election was firmly on soothing the anxieties of the middle and upper classes and ensuring that the wealth class remained unprovoked.

Perhaps elections in Australia had always revolved around appeasing the middle class, promising hip-pocket relief to keep them onboard and worshipping the Gods of neoliberalism, but it felt like this focus had become stronger and more performative in recent elections. It was a continuation of a strategy that dated back to Robert Menzies' iconic 1942 'forgotten people' speech, where he positioned the middle class as the moral centre of Australia—the self-reliant, stoic citizens who neither sought nor required government assistance. Menzies' portrayal resonated because the middle class was expanding at that time, driven by suburban growth from the 1920s and 1930s, accelerating after World War II. However, since the neoliberal era—and particularly under John Howard—the middle class steadily shrank.

By 2025, a lingering aspiration persisted, one that mirrored American mythology: the belief that poverty was only temporary, and even the struggling classes were simply 'embarrassed millionaires' awaiting their turn at prosperity if they worked hard enough, a belief cynically weaponised during the election campaign. The Coalition's promises of tax cuts for the wealthy—in conjunction with their message that living today was like a dystopian Dickensian era—were pitched not just to the rich but also to those who imagined that, someday soon, they too would be wealthy. It was a politics built on aspiration and illusion, exploiting the dream that self-interest today would be rewarded with affluence tomorrow. In the meantime, the real and more uncomfortable truth—that wealth was concentrating ever upwards while economic vulnerability spread downwards—was drowned out by the relentless clatter of the manufactured cost of living panic.

LEADERS FUELLED COST OF LIVING PANIC WITHOUT SOLVING IT

Throughout the election campaign, neither major party focused on real solutions for those most impacted by poverty and economic hardship. There was almost complete silence on increasing JobSeeker payments, assisting the unemployed, addressing youth unemployment, or improving the lives of people living in poverty. It was as if the prevailing mindset, echoing the harshest aspects of the American system, was that anyone in economic distress must have failed personally and, because of this, was unworthy of political attention. As had been the pattern for decades, the entire election narrative remained tightly locked on hip-pocket issues and financial aspirations for those already doing relatively well.

The media's constant hammering about a 'cost of living crisis' predominantly for the middle and upper classes created a feedback loop: the more it was emphasised, the more these groups demanded government action to protect their lifestyles, and the more political leaders responded by funnelling benefits and relief to them—largely ignoring the needs of lower-income and vulnerable groups. While some support did reach disadvantaged areas, the overwhelming majority of political promises and media attention remained firmly directed at middle- and upper-income Australians. This created a dangerous illusion that everyone could and would become financially secure if only they voted a certain way, reinforcing a myth of endless upward mobility.

The old promises of trickle-down economics still lingered. But with this illusion of the 'trickle-down' effect, the problem wasn't that the flow eventually went past the brim and reached those below—it was that when the flow got closer to the top, it was simply replaced with a larger vessel: the promised trickle never appeared, the accumulation remained at the top. It's a brutal but accurate depiction of how political and economic structures evolved.

The result was a deepening disillusionment with both major parties, fuelling record levels of informal voting and disengagement, especially among those who saw their real issues—secure jobs, affordable housing, accessible healthcare—being ignored. Tax cuts for the wealthy? No problem. Defence spending? Unlimited. Higher education and Medicare? Pushed to the background.

The Labor Party made a pledge to reinvest in Medicare, a modest but critical attempt to reverse the hollowing-out that took place under the Abbott, Turnbull and Morrison governments. Australia's public healthcare system is one of the best in the world, but increasingly under strain, and Labor's commitment, if followed through and supported by any crossbench alliances if needed, could help preserve and even rebuild it. By contrast, Dutton offered no serious proposals to strengthen Medicare—perhaps unsurprising given that when he served as Health Minister in 2013–14, he was infamously voted by *Australian Doctor* magazine as the worst health minister in Australia's history.

It spoke volumes about the political priorities on offer in the election: a contest not about addressing real structural inequality, but about which side could better manage the anxieties of the comfortable classes while leaving the root causes of hardship untouched.

WHERE THE REAL COST OF LIVING CRISIS HAS AN IMPACT

If the election was framed as the 'cost of living election', it was worth stepping back from the noise and looking at the reality behind the slogans and the avalanche of media messaging. While the media kept pushing the message of a 'crisis', the economic data offered a more complicated story. The consumer price index had gone down to 2.4 per cent, a significant decline from its peak of 7.8 per cent in 2022. The wage price index, which tracks growth in income levels, had risen to 3.2 per cent, the highest since 2009. Retail turnover had gone up by 8 per cent since May 2022, and overseas travel had almost returned to pre-COVID levels, with international trips and holidays reaching 95 per cent of the volume in 2019.

Yes, there were many financial pressures, especially for mortgage holders and renters, who saw significant rises in repayments and rental costs over the past three years. However, overall consumer sentiment painted a more gloomy picture than the statistics suggested—there was a mismatch between the economic data and public feeling, a gap that the media played a large role in widening. The repetitive media depiction of a 'cost of living crisis' created an atmosphere of fear and pessimism that was not entirely borne out by the figures. Media monitoring suggests a pattern: when a Coalition government is in office, national debt, inflation, and price pressures are often underreported or downplayed. When a Labor government is in power, these issues are pushed to the foreground, portrayed as existential crises regardless of the actual trends.

That was not to say there wasn't a real cost of living issue—there was. But the crisis was not uniform across society. Middle- and upper-income households generally weathered the storm well, continuing to spend, travel, and maintain lifestyles, while lower-income households genuinely struggled. It was among these lower-income groups where the real cost of living pain was concentrated, and neither Labor nor the Coalition showed much appetite to address it in any systemic or transformative way.

This was where the electoral impact was likely to be felt by the government. In the traditional Labor strongholds—outer suburban electorates where mortgage stress, rent rises, and stagnant real wages hit the hardest—discontent simmered. This was a situation reflected in the 2022 Victorian state election, where large swings occurred in safe Labor seats in the outer Melbourne suburban ring, but not enough to lose those seats. This didn't end up costing Labor government federally, as the expected swings did not eventuate, but it is an issue that they will need to focus on in future elections.

During the campaign, the Liberal Party aggressively targeted these outer suburban areas, aware that their path back to power depended on winning over struggling families who felt abandoned. Yet despite the credible work of some local Liberal candidates, the Coalition's broader problem remained: a lack of credible national leadership and a vision that could unite and inspire.

Without a strong central leadership offering a compelling alternative to the public, it was difficult to see the Coalition making the kinds of breakthroughs it needed to fundamentally change the election's outcome. The cost of living narrative might have been powerful—but it wasn't powerful enough to overcome leadership deficits.

CULTURE WARS AND THE POLITICS OF DESPERATION

As the final week of the campaign wore on, Anthony Albanese and the Labor government remained firmly focused on cost of living pressures—reinforcing their record on inflation control, wage growth, and targeted relief measures. For Peter Dutton and the Liberal Party, however, the terrain was far more treacherous. They attempted to amplify cost of living concerns but struggled to connect with voters or present a compelling alternative. So, in the absence of substantive policy ideas or a credible plan for economic relief, the campaign once again veered into the comforting chaos of culture war politics.

That descent had started at the end of the previous week when a Welcome to Country ceremony at Melbourne's ANZAC Day commemorations was interrupted by hecklers—later revealed to be organised Neo-Nazi agitators. The moment was ugly and disturbing on its own terms, but even more concerning was the link to Advance Australia, a far-right lobbying group bankrolled by Liberal Party donors. This tactic—provocation in the service of electoral advantage—echoed the strategy used during the 2023 Voice to Parliament referendum. The parallels were unmistakable: when there's nothing left to offer, fall back on division and wedge politics. And this time, unlike the Voice referendum, it appeared to have backfired.

The idea seemed to be that the manufactured outrage over Welcome to Country ceremonies would stir up the same kind of populist anger that had sunk the Voice. But what worked in the context of a polarising referendum didn't translate to a general election, especially one that voters increasingly saw through the lens of their wallets. The playbook from 2023 was dusted off and thrown back into the election campaign—but Australians, it seemed, weren't buying it. If this sort of nonsense really had been enough to swing the entire election, then political journalism in this country would have needed to admit it had fundamentally misunderstood the electorate. But all signs suggested otherwise. As in 2022, when Scott Morrison resorted to transphobic dog-whistling in the final weeks of a dying campaign, the Liberal Party once again reached for cultural resentment in the absence of policy direction. It didn't work in 2022, and it didn't work in 2025.

What's perhaps most remarkable was not that the Liberal Party resorted to the same tactics—it's that they expected it to work again. They learned all the wrong lessons from their referendum win, mistaking a protest vote against an incoherent "Yes" campaign for a blanket endorsement of their politics. Meanwhile, Labor took the opposite path—recognising the dangers of misinformation and learning to fight fire with clarity. This time around, they were ready for the lies, and they neutralised them early and effectively.

A CAMPAIGN TO SAVE THE ELECTORAL FURNITURE

The final days were marked not by a final persuasive push from the Liberal Party, but by a clumsy and at times menacing overreach. Across key electorates, the party attempted to overwhelm the polling booths—not with ideas or vision—but with sheer physical presence. In electorates such as Kooyong in Melbourne and Reid in Sydney, Liberal campaigners blanketed pre-polling centres with corflutes, A-frames, and personnel. In some cases, their signage even spilled onto the roadways, requiring council intervention to have it removed for safety reasons. It was a display not of enthusiasm, but of desperation—a kind of visual assault that smacked of panic rather than professionalism.

The tactic backfired. Far from projecting strength, the relentless branding, bullying behaviour, and saturation of volunteers created an atmosphere of hostility. In Reid, voters encountered not just large numbers of Liberal volunteers, but aggressive ones—many of whom were later revealed not to be party members at all, but activists from the Exclusive Brethren, a secretive religious sect whose members, for religious reasons, do not even vote in elections. The message this sent was clear: the Liberal Party was willing to flood polling booths with ideological shock troops, even if they weren't part of the democratic process. Instead of convincing voters, the display alienated them. This intimidation at the ballot box did not win support—it repelled it. The Liberal Party failed to win in Kooyong; in Reid, the sitting Labor member, Sally Sitou, increased her two-party preferred vote by 6.7 per cent.

In these final stages, the contrast between the media strategies of the two major party leaders could not have been more different.

Albanese appeared at the National Press Club and fielded a wide range of questions from all corners of the mainstream media. Peter Dutton, by contrast, largely retreated into the comfort of right-wing echo chambers, refusing to engage with broad-based media and labelling the ABC and *The Guardian* as "hate media". In a campaign where reaching undecided voters and moderates was critical, Dutton's decision to limit his appearances to Sky News and 2GB was politically self-defeating.

Rather than show leadership and openness, Dutton doubled down on hostility. His attacks on the media were not only petulant—they exposed a deeper insecurity about the Coalition's lack of cut-through. His fiery speech to party faithful, urging them to "forget what you're being told by the ABC and *The Guardian*," sounded more like a conspiracy theorist's rallying cry than the words of a serious candidate for national leadership. And when offered the softest of interviews by Sky News' Shari Markson, Dutton did what became routine in his campaign—complained about media bias, played the victim, and railed against "inner-city green voters" without offering much in the way of policy or leadership.

For a leader who claimed to represent mainstream values and middle Australia, Dutton's deliberate media isolation was revealing. Refusing to engage with the ABC during an election campaign—particularly when it remains one of the more trusted sources of news in the country—was not a strategy for winning new voters; it was an act of surrender. Worse still was his bizarre directive for supporters to boycott the ABC on election night, presumably so they wouldn't have to hear the psephologist

Antony Green declare yet another loss for the Coalition. It was petty, it was graceless, and it reeked of defeat.

This failure wasn't just about media optics—it was strategic. Dutton's campaign was conceived and executed within a shrinking ideological bubble. Instead of reaching out to undecided voters and the broader public through diverse media channels—including podcasts, online platforms, independent outlets, and even hostile programs—he clung to Sky News and right-wing radio, mistaking volume for reach and sycophancy for strategy. As a result, he never built the public momentum required to turn around the polls. He spoke to the converted while ignoring the voters he needed to win.

In contrast, Albanese learned from the mistakes of the 2022 campaign. He understood that elections are won not by preaching to your base but by engaging with the undecided middle. That meant fronting tough questions, enduring criticism, and showing up in spaces that weren't always friendly. Dutton chose the opposite path—and in doing so, undermined his own legitimacy as a prospective national leader.

There's a reason successful leaders—Howard, Keating, Rudd—embraced the cut and thrust of media interrogation. It wasn't just political theatre; it was a public test of character and composure. Dutton failed that test. As the final week dragged on and into into the final days, it became clear that the Liberal campaign wasn't trying to win—it was preparing for the clean-up. And Dutton, the leader who walked into a trap of his own making, seemed destined to be the last casualty of a dying political era.

REMEMBERING THE GHOSTS OF 2019

The skies across Australia were mostly clear on May 3, yet there remained a whisper from the ghosts of elections past—a lingering phantom that threatened to upend the day's expectations and somehow deliver a result favouring the conservative forces across the land. Election day had finally arrived, and as the final votes were placed into ballot boxes across the nation, the last round of opinion polling confirmed the consistent message that had emerged throughout the campaign: Labor was on track to win the 2025 federal election.

Whether it secured a majority or fell just short and governed in minority was confirmed late on Saturday night—a clear majority—but across the major pollsters—Newspoll, Resolve, Essential, Morgan, YouGov, and Demos—the two-party-preferred range sat between 52–48 per cent and 53–47 per cent in Labor's favour. There was no late swing, no surge of momentum for the Liberal–National Coalition, and certainly no tangible sign that a 'miracle victory' was brewing. But despite this consistency, the ghosts of the 2019 federal election still hovered in the background of this election.

REMEMBERING THE GHOSTS OF 2019

In 2019, opinion polls predicted a Labor victory under Bill Shorten. Instead, Scott Morrison stunned observers with a narrow but decisive win, proving just how wrong the polling industry could sometimes be. But there were a few critical differences between 2019 and 2025—differences that reduced the chances of another upset result.

The most critical issue was the campaign performance itself—Peter Dutton ran what was widely regarded as a disastrous campaign: reactive, negative, undisciplined, and disconnected from the political centre. In contrast, Anthony Albanese ran a steady, if unspectacular, campaign defined by competence and clarity. There were no major scandals, no self-inflicted wounds—except perhaps for a momentary media frenzy over Albanese's minor fall at a public event. If that was the worst controversy of Labor's five-week effort, then it was a sign of a campaign that stuck to the plan and delivered the message.

Polling firms, too, had learned from their mistakes. After the methodological failures of 2019, many recalibrated how they sampled, weighted, and analysed voter sentiment—particularly around undecided voters and disengaged demographics. While pollsters remained cautious and always warned that their polls were not predictions but snapshots at a given time, they also acknowledged that consistent polling across all firms this close to election day usually signalled a reliable outcome—at least in terms of the likely winner, if not the precise seat tally.

More importantly, Peter Dutton was not Scott Morrison. He entered the final week with a net approval rating of minus 24 points, far worse than Shorten's minus 8 points at the same stage in 2019. Albanese's approval rating was plus 1 point—identical to Morrison's rating in the lead-up to his surprise victory. For Dutton to have replicated that 2019 'miracle' victory, he would at least have needed to be in Albanese's position. Instead, he was in a far worse place than even the losing candidate from 2019.

Another structural disadvantage for Dutton was that he was trying to win from opposition. The political fortunes tended to favour incumbent governments, especially first-term ones, unless there was widespread dissatisfaction. But Albanese's administration, while not immune to criticism, largely avoided scandal, delivered economic stability, and presented a unified front. Cabinet unity was tight; while there was a cabinet reshuffle in 2024, no ministers resigned in disgrace; no leaks derailed the campaign. The same could not be said for the Liberal Party, where internal players continued to leak stories to the media and, in some cases, directly to the Labor Party itself.

While both major parties brought out the ghosts of 2019 in different ways—Labor as a cautionary message against complacency; the Coalition as a call to faith and belief in electoral miracles—the context had changed and the political landscape was quite different. The leaders were different. And the electorate was different. Voters were more engaged in the pre-polling process, with nearly half the electorate having already cast a ballot before election day. That shifting dynamic made last-minute momentum harder to generate, and harder still to measure.

It was also worth noting that the 2019 opinion polling errors were not as catastrophic as often portrayed—while the figures were incorrect, the result was still within the margin of error, but the opinion polls miscalculated where that error would land.

This time around, every major pollster showed a clear Labor lead—albeit a narrow one in some cases. For all of them to have been wrong, again, and in the same direction, would have represented an extraordinary statistical anomaly.

In the end, opinion polls aren't the cause of an election win or loss, but they do provide a barometer of where the public mood is heading. And by election day, that barometer pointed toward a second term for Anthony Albanese. If Peter Dutton had somehow won from so far behind, it would not simply have been a comeback—it would have been a political resurrection of unprecedented proportions. But the numbers didn't lie: an unpopular leader, a faltering campaign, a fractured party, and a hostile public mood all pointed in one direction. Unless something extraordinary occurred at the eleventh hour, the Coalition's hope mainly lay in saving enough of the political furniture to rebuild—and, more than likely, under new leadership.

ELECTION DAY: THE RECKONING

And so, it had come to this: after five weeks of campaigning, political theatre, strategic missteps, and moments of occasional clarity, we reached the most important part of the campaign: the closing of the polling booths and the counting of the votes in the 2025 federal election. And while it was always wise to be cautious—especially with the spectre of 2019 threatening to disrupt these predictions—the political landscape, polling data, and the campaigns themselves all pointed to one likely result: a Labor victory, most probably in majority government.

There were many reasons for this prediction, and most of them were rooted not in soaring support for Labor, but in the dismal performance of the Coalition. Albanese's government, while far from perfect, had been stable, competent, and relatively scandal-free. The public perception of Labor was bolstered by a sense of steadiness, economic management, and ministerial unity. Even its political failings—such as its lacklustre housing policy, an underwhelming anti-corruption commission, and its cowardice on the genocide committed by Israel in Palestine—did not translate into a widespread voter backlash. These issues weighed heavily on progressives and political observers, but for most of the electorate, they didn't define the government.

On the other side, Dutton's campaign was relentlessly negative, often chaotic, and completely devoid of compelling vision, and the Coalition failed to articulate a clear reason for voters to turf out a first-term government. And to run a negative campaign successfully, a party had to be disciplined, precise, and highly strategic—none of which described what we witnessed from the Coalition during the five-week campaign. Simply turning up during a campaign with a relentless megaphone of negativity rarely won an election: voters needed a positive light and direction for where the country was heading over the next three years.

The late release of the Coalition's policy costings—on the penultimate day of the campaign—reinforced this sense of disorder and gave the media and electorate no time to evaluate them, with just the vague promise of being "$10 billion better off," in conjunction with a final photo-op at the petrol bowser to push a promised 50 per cent reduction in excise. Petrol prices had actually fallen by around 15 per cent since the last election; this focus on petrol prices was a misstep—yet another sign of a campaign looking for quick stunts rather than serious substance. Dutton's personal unpopularity dogged him during the entire campaign and he was the least liked major party leader in polling history heading into a federal election.

At the point when the polling booths closed, the final analysis of the election was clear: the Coalition could not realistically reach the 76-seat threshold needed to form a majority. It is equally unlikely they could form a minority government. That path would have required a miraculous confluence of preference flows, independent crossbench support, and a primary vote that simply wasn't there. While isolated upsets can occur on election night, the idea of a Dutton-led Coalition negotiating a path to government in this political climate was bordering on fantasy.

In contrast, it appeared that the independent and minor party vote would continue to reshape Australian politics. The crossbench appeared likely to remain large—even in the event of a Labor majority. Most community independents were expected to retain their seats, particularly those in affluent, formerly Liberal electorates. The teal independents who defeated Morrison-era conservatives were unlikely to see voters return to the even more regressive Peter Dutton.

The Australia Greens were also to expected to increase their lower house representation, although whether an expected higher primary vote could translate into seat gains remained uncertain. As was witnessed in the 2024 Queensland state election, their primary vote could actually rise nationally but could also concentrate in places where they were already strong, yielding little net change.

However, Australians had sent signals in recent elections that they wanted better representation, more integrity, and less of the tribal culture war politics that defined the Morrison and now Dutton era. And if the outcome reflected what the polls and campaigns had suggested, this election confirmed that the public remained on that trajectory—and that the Liberal Party, as it was then constituted, was not part of that future. All that remained was for the Australian Electoral Commission to do its work and count the votes to see if this would be proven correct.

ELECTION NIGHT: A HISTORIC VICTORY AND A DEVASTATING LOSS

No-one really expected this. There were murmurs, some wishful thinking, a few outlandish predictions—but few expected this incredibly one-sided outcome. And yet, many of those wild claims were realised. While a number of seats on election night still remained too close to call, their outcome would do little to change the broader picture: the Albanese Labor government had not only retained power—it had expanded its majority to that of a *landslide*. On election night, Jim Chalmers' attempts to suppress his delight on the ABC broadcast were only partially successful, while Liberal Senator James McGrath did a 'Chemical Ali' job of avoiding awkward questions about his party's crumbling prospects, constantly suggesting that it was best to wait for more votes to come in, even though it was obvious to everyone that result was well and truly decided.

Perhaps the most striking moment of the evening came not from the winners, but the vanquished: Peter Dutton's concession speech was unexpectedly gracious. It was humble, even self-deprecating—he accepted full responsibility for the loss, acknowledged the personal journey of his opponent with an empathetic nod to Anthony Albanese's late mother, and gave his blessing to the incoming Labor MP in his former seat, Ali France. For a man whose political brand had for years been associated with hostility, authoritarianism and culture war skirmishes, the moment was disarming. This was not the Peter Dutton the electorate had come to know: it didn't undo years of his political brutality, but it did offer a note of dignity to what was likely the closing chapter of his political career.

The magnitude of the Liberal defeat, and the momentary humanity of Dutton's departure, calls to mind another dramatic reckoning: the election of 1943. The United Australia Party—a precursor to today's Liberal Party—suffered a historic loss at the hands of John Curtin's Labor Party. Like the Liberal Party of 2025, the UAP had once been dominant, governing from 1931 to 1940 under the leadership of Joe Lyons. But Lyons' death, and the flawed elevation of the young and unpopular Robert Menzies, precipitated a rapid decline. Menzies, too arrogant for the times, was soon forced to resign, retreating to the backbench in disgrace. The UAP floundered under ageing and uninspiring leadership, was seen as a servant of big business, and had become disconnected from the national mood.

The parallels are remarkable: a party led by unpopular and ill-suited leaders. A steady exodus of moderates. A loss of identity created by years of ideological games. The 1943 election wasn't just a defeat—it was an existential crisis. Menzies, to his credit, recognised this. In 1944, with a mix of business and conservative allies, he created a new party: the Liberal Party of Australia. It would spend the next several decades dominating Australian politics, with only a few interruptions.

That success now feels like ancient history. The modern Liberal Party has purged its moderate flank. The last remaining centrists, Bridget Archer and Keith Wolahan, were swept away in the election night Labor surge through Tasmania and Melbourne. Calls for introspection during these moments are usually drowned out by demands to shift 'further to the right'—a strategy that continues to produce diminishing returns, not just federally, but in state and local contests. Outside its echo chamber, the Liberal Party's alignment with the fringe ideas of the Institute of Public Affairs is toxic. And much like the UAP of the 1940s, the Liberal Party of 2025 is beginning to resemble a political museum relic—one that needs reinvention and replacement, to remain relevant in an Australia that has long since moved on.

LABOR'S DISCIPLINE, CONSISTENCY AND THE POWER OF INCUMBENCY

While the Liberal Party unravelled under the weight of internal discord, miscalculation, and ideology, the Labor Party ran one of the most disciplined and effective campaigns in recent memory. It wasn't flashy. It wasn't revolutionary. But it was relentlessly consistent, grounded in pragmatic messaging, and focused on projecting stability—exactly what a risk-averse electorate seemed to want in 2025.

Labor understood the strength of incumbency and used it carefully. Anthony Albanese positioned himself not as a radical reformer, but as a steady hand during uncertain times. His campaign leaned on achievements: real wage growth, declining inflation, a strengthened Medicare system, and modest gains in housing affordability—presented not as *solved crises*, but as challenges being actively and competently managed. It was a subtle, yet powerful narrative: *we know things aren't perfect—but trust us, they're getting better.*

Critically, Labor resisted the temptation to overreach during the campaign. While the Liberal campaign descended into increasingly dystopian warnings about national collapse and social decay, Labor stuck to measured optimism. Albanese avoided major gaffes, kept controversial ministers largely out of the spotlight, and maintained a clear focus on kitchen-table issues: wages, health, cost of living, and economic certainty. Rather than getting drawn into culture war traps set by the Coalition—on nuclear power, race, gender, and immigration—Labor avoided them altogether. It was a deliberate and disciplined campaign, one that left the Coalition shouting into a void while the electorate turned away.

DUTTON'S UNDOING: MISSTEPS, MISJUDGEMENTS AND ALIENATION

Dutton's defeat was not the result of a single event or tactical blunder—it was the culmination of choices over the years that alienated the very voters he needed to win over. Much had been made of Dutton's overt embrace of Trump-style politics, from the hardline nationalism and race-baiting dog whistles to the stifling culture war rhetoric that felt increasingly imported from the worst of American public debate. But as the United States continued its slide into dysfunction, many Australian voters took a long, hard look and decided this was not an agenda they wanted to follow.

The more immediate blunder came even before the campaign commenced, when Cyclone Alfred struck Queensland. While

ELECTION NIGHT: A HISTORIC VICTORY AND A DEVASTATING LOSS

thousands of residents braced for damage and disruption, Dutton—whose own electorate of Dickson was affected—chose to leave the state for a fundraising event in Sydney, surrounded by corporate donors and political elites. The optics were devastating: the man who wanted to lead the country appeared to abandon his constituents at a moment of crisis. Even for voters who may have tolerated his abrasive style, this act of detachment seemed to be a final breach of trust. For many in the seat of Dickson, this was the moment Dutton forfeited the right to represent them.

But his real downfall may have started much earlier, during the 2023 Voice to Parliament referendum. Dutton's decision to lead the "No" campaign was, at the time, widely seen as a political gamble—a chance to rally the base, weaponise division, and further isolate Labor from conservative and regional Australia. The campaign succeeded in defeating the Voice proposal, but the victory came at a steep cost. Public sentiment shifted rapidly in the months that followed. Voters—particularly younger Australians, women, Indigenous communities, and urban moderates—began to view the "No" campaign as rooted in deception, fearmongering, and barely concealed racial undertones. Dutton became the face of that campaign, and for many Australians, he came to embody a form of politics they no longer wished to be associated with.

Perception became reality. Even if Dutton was not personally racist—and by all accounts, many colleagues insisted he is not—the image was indelibly stamped. The political stain was compounded by his dry, often sarcastic manner, which read less as wit and more as disdain. For younger voters and women especially, Dutton's style felt combative and cold. He was a man out of step with the country he wished to lead.

In the end, Dutton's concession speech revealed much about his political journey. He made no mention of his leadership, his years in opposition, or even his electorate. Instead, he claimed his career highlight was his time as defence minister—a position built on security, militarism, and fortress politics. It was an interesting admission: for a man who led his party through one of its worst defeats in decades—if not *the* worst—and who could never quite shake his image as a political enforcer, there was no prime ministerial grace note waiting for him. Just the final irony of a career defined by division, ending in a moment of unexpected humility. Dutton wasn't beaten by fate—he was, in many ways, destined never to lead.

REBUILDING THE LIBERAL PARTY

By any sober measure, the Coalition was never going to win the 2025 election. Requiring a net gain of twenty-two seats, the path to majority government was just a mathematical fantasy. But that doesn't mean the campaign had to be wasted in this way. A smarter opposition could have used this parliamentary term to consolidate its base, target winnable seats, and prepare a compelling policy vision that could lay the basis for the next election in 2028. Instead, the Liberal Party drifted through the campaign with policy offerings and costings that were weak and barely held up to scrutiny, vague promises, and a strategy that seemed to rely more on media favours and culture-wars outrage than on genuine public engagement.

While Labor presented discipline, consistency, and policy credibility, the Liberal campaign often looked like a disorganised imitation of past mistakes. The old trick of 'muddling through'—which had worked to a degree in 2013, 2016 and 2019—had finally run its course. The political landscape had changed, and the Liberal Party hadn't kept up. In contrast, Labor had done the hard internal work: it cleared out underperformers, reconciled internal factional tensions, refined its policy program, and learned the lessons from the 2019 defeat and the Voice referendum debacle with a more cohesive, future-oriented identity.

The Liberal Party, by contrast, lacked discipline, clarity, and self-awareness. It seemed complacent—still convinced that culture war slogans and reactionary talking points could substitute for substance and be enough to win. Where Labor had learned and adapted, the Liberals had regressed. It no longer knew who it was fighting for. Menzies once spoke to "the forgotten people"—the middle class that felt ignored by elites and the working class alike. John Howard found resonance with "Howard's battlers"—aspirational blue-collar voters. Even Tony Abbott's crude appeal to "Tony's tradies" had, for a time, connected with a segment of the electorate.

Dutton's Liberals, however, built their identity around a hollow rejection: they were *not* woke, *not* elite, *not* educated. They defined themselves by opposition—against imagined enemies rather than for real constituents. But these enemies were never clearly defined, and the concerns they obsessed over bore little relation to the actual anxieties of the electorate. With cost-of-living pressures, housing insecurity, interest rate worries, and international instability front of mind, the Coalition chose to shout about gender identity and 'cancel culture'. *Anti-woke.* The disconnect was profound. And it was *political suicide.*

The Liberal Party now enters what could be a long, painful period of introspection—or further denial. What is required is nothing short of a Menzies-style reimagination. When Menzies founded the Liberal Party in 1944, he correctly identified a growing middle class that wanted stability, autonomy, and dignity. But that middle class—stable, secure, upwardly mobile—has all but vanished in contemporary Australia. A new Liberal Party will have to look more deeply, and honestly, at what Australia is now: fractured by inequality, energised by diversity, and far less tolerant of dogma. This party must shape itself not for a fantasy electorate, but for the real one that exists today—and govern with a vision that appeals beyond donors, media backers, and culture warriors.

The right has failed to do this for decades. If it cannot now, the Liberal Party may fade into the same irrelevance that consumed the United Australia Party before it. While we can't focus too much on the losers in this election—this is a one-in-a-generation type of victory for the Labor Party and must be savoured as much as possible by their supporters—how the Liberal Party rebuilds itself will be one of the fascinating narratives of this next parliamentary term.

THE COLLAPSE OF A PARTY: WHAT'S NEXT FOR THE LIBERALS?

If a federal election produced a once-in-a-generation victory for one side of politics, it usually came with a matching catastrophe on the other side—and that's exactly what unfolded for the Liberal–National Coalition in the 2025 election. The scale of the Liberal Party's defeat was unprecedented in Australian political history, and it was difficult to see how the party could quickly return to political respectability. Peter Dutton, delivering a sombre and funereal concession speech, acknowledged this reality with a tone of resignation on election night: "Tonight's not the night that we wanted... but we've worked hard every day over the course of the last three years to do our best for our amazing country". These were hollow words in the face of the devastating results—both for the Liberal Party and for Dutton personally, who became the first sitting opposition leader in federal history to lose his own seat at a general election.

This wasn't just a bad night for the Coalition; it was a *political disaster*. The primary vote collapsed to 32 per cent, the lowest ever recorded for the Coalition, and the two-party-preferred vote sank to 45.2 per cent—another record low. They managed to secure just forty-two seats, with the Nationals holding steady (fifteen seats), while the Liberal Party bore the full brunt of voter dissatisfaction. Sixteen seats were lost by the Liberal Party; its campaign was weak, uninspiring, and incoherent, and the leadership of Dutton and his deputy, Sussan Ley—widely considered tone-deaf and out of touch—received a terrible verdict from the electorate.

The Liberal Party's collapse was severe in the urban heartlands that once defined its base. The party lost its footing in both inner and outer metropolitan areas, transforming what was once a powerful national political force into a party with diminishing urban relevance—something that looked like a second-tier regional organisation, trailing behind even the Nationals in coherence and purpose. Such an electoral wipe-out not only made a comeback in 2028 virtually impossible, but also raised the possibility that the party would not return to power until the 2030s—if then. It was quite possible that the next Liberal Party Prime Minister hadn't yet walked through the doors of Parliament—or even signed their party membership form.

The causes of this collapse will be openly debated and carefully dissected, even among the party's traditional supporters. For years, the Liberal Party had followed a political and ideological compass that pointed sharply to the right—egged on by the Murdoch media and figures such as Paul Murray and Peta Credlin. Yet in moving further into the culture-war wilderness, the party abandoned the very people it was originally created to represent. Formed in 1944 as an urban and suburban middle-class party, the Liberal Party had lost not only traditional strongholds like Kooyong, Deakin, Wentworth and Mackellar, but also the outer-suburban aspirational seats that often decide elections. While the seat of Goldstein in Melbourne had been clawed back, and Kooyong came close, it wasn't nearly enough to offset the collapse elsewhere.

Even conservative commentators admitted the party must urgently refocus on urban Australia or risk permanent political irrelevance. The Coalition might be intact in name, but the Liberal Party's soul—and its pathway back to national leadership—had never been in greater doubt.

THE CULTURE WARS THAT ATE THE LIBERAL PARTY

The Liberal Party's catastrophic defeat in the 2025 federal election wasn't just a rejection of its campaign or leader—it was a rejection of an entire political identity that had decayed over the past thirty years. This election felt less like a change of government and more like a mass flushing of the political drain—an emphatic rejection of the hard-right, culture-war-driven politics that had defined the Liberal Party since the Howard era. What began in the mid-1990s as a purge of moderates and a consolidation around conservative values had finally reached its logical endpoint: irrelevance in the very electorates that once formed the backbone of Liberal power.

Then a dangerous complacency set in: the Coalition convinced itself that, because it had managed to scrape through elections in 2016 and 2019—largely with the aid of fear campaigns, divisive rhetoric, and political luck—it could keep reusing the same formula indefinitely. When it lost the election in 2022, it treated the result as a temporary setback rather than a structural warning and, instead of recalibrating its offerings to the public, it doubled down. Instead of reflecting, it retreated further into its ideological bunker. Rather than modernising or making peace with shifting social norms and community expectations, the Liberal Party continued to indulge in reactionary tantrums—on race, gender, Indigenous issues, and immigration—hoping that the outrage would mask its deficiencies in policy development.

And still, after the thumping loss in 2025, some within the party's ranks were pushing for *more* of the same. Immediately after the election, Sky News' Rita Panahi and former party vice-president Teena McQueen became outraged by the party's supposed slide toward "Labor-lite" politics, framing the failure not as a result of Dutton's relentless negativity or lack of vision, but as a consequence of him not being *right-wing enough*. McQueen lamented that the executive was "spooked" into softening their messaging on areas such as immigration and Welcome to Country announcements—as if doubling down on Trump-style culture wars could have saved the campaign. That this sort of commentary still finds a receptive audience within the party is a clear indication of how disconnected it has become from mainstream Australia.

At many levels, the Liberal Party appeared dysfunctional. While it held power in Queensland, Tasmania, and the Northern Territory at a state and territory level, these were anomalies rather than signs of vitality. Federally, it had become a hollowed-out shell: bereft of ideas, devoid of vision, and addicted to wedge politics. There was no forward-looking agenda, no appeal to the future—just an endless recycling of fear, resentment, and scapegoating. Its targets were predictable and uninspiring: attacks on the left and "wokeness," Indigenous communities, migrants, China, and anyone vaguely "different"—*the other*. And yet somehow, the party leadership seemed to think a narrow win in Goldstein or a near-miss in Kooyong justified staying the hardline course. But this was false hope built on fragile foundations. If Tim Wilson was considered a core part of the party's future, it really seemed like a bleak future. His record as a local member in Goldstein was marred by controversy, arrogance, and underperformance—hardly a signpost for renewal.

At the heart of the matter was a crisis of purpose. The Liberal Party no longer seemed to know what it stood for, beyond the protection of its own elite and the preservation of privilege. Certainly, the wealthy classes deserve representation, like everyone else in the community, but the seats they hold at the table are far bigger than everyone else's. Once a mainstream party fails to listen to and reflect the broad interests of the electorate, it ceases to be a mainstream party: it morphs into a niche faction masquerading as a movement. In refusing to listen—to *really* listen—to the Australian public, the Liberal Party had revealed its own insularity and denial.

A LEADERSHIP VACUUM IN THE POLITICAL WRECKAGE

With Dutton losing his seat, the Liberal Party ended the election not just demoralised but without a leader—and without a clear pathway forward. What remained of its leadership aspirants was uninspiring at best. The contest for the top job after the election narrowed down to Angus Taylor, who was the Shadow Treasurer, and Sussan Ley. Senator Jacinta Price, who had defected from the National Party room to the Liberal Party after the election, also placed herself on a joint ticket with Taylor—even though she'd only been in the party for less than a week—a move that didn't go down well with more established and longer-term members of the Liberal Party.

There were also murmurings that Wilson, after narrowly winning the seat of Goldstein, would raise his hand for the leadership contest, but this didn't eventuate. Of course, every party needs to have a leader, but even discussing leadership at this point felt like a pointless exercise—a distraction from the deeper existential work the party must do to avoid long-term irrelevance. In the end, Sussan Ley became the leader of the Liberal Party in a close party room vote—29 votes to Taylor's 25—with the member for Fairfax, Ted O'Brien, elected as deputy leader. And upon assuming the leadership, Ley once again accused the Prime Minister of fuelling anti-Semitism, claiming that his approach to Jewish Australians was "one of the biggest threats to social cohesion". Within an hour of appointing a new leader, the Liberal Party had shown it had learned nothing from its election loss, even though the clamour of its largest electoral defeat was still reverberating.

But this wasn't just about choosing a new figurehead. It was about rebuilding from the ground up—something the party should have begun after its defeat in 2022 but stubbornly refused to address. The Liberal Party had shrunk to a conservative rump: of the forty-two seats retained by the Coalition, only twenty-seven belonged to the Liberals. Their identity was fractured, their membership base ageing, and their unbreakable connections to bodies such as the Institute of Public Affairs and media echo chambers like Sky News and News Corporation had stifled any capacity for genuine renewal. These partnerships might once have served as sources of influence and policy development, but they now acted more like ideological anchors, dragging the party away from mainstream Australia.

The scale of the rebuild ahead is massive—and might not bear fruit for a decade or more. While it's unwise to rule out anything in politics—remembering that Labor returned to office in 2007 after the 2004 electoral wipeout—the 2028 election already seemed out of reach. Even 2031 felt optimistic. It might be 2034 before the Liberals could seriously think about forming government again. But to get there, the party needed to undertake a brutal reassessment of what it is, who it represents in the electorate, and whether it can be something more than a political receptacle for resentment and privilege.

Right now, after a comprehensive election loss, it didn't matter who the leader was—Taylor, Ley, Wilson, Price, or some other unknown figure. The party needed to stop obsessing over personalities and start doing the hard background work it had neglected for many years. Policy development, community engagement, renewal of local branches, and outreach beyond the ideological base of young hyperactive MAGA wannabes and crusty old men who think *political correctness has gone mad*—these are the fundamentals the party had failed to invest in. Dutton was, at best, always going to be a leadership placeholder, and though his exit from Parliament spared him the brunt of internal blame, his legacy was one of strategic failure and political delusion. That he genuinely believed the commentary from Sky News about his prime ministerial destiny only highlighted how deeply cut off from reality the leadership had become.

Looking back, this trajectory had been long in the making. After John Howard purged the party of moderates in the mid-'90s, a pattern emerged. Tony Abbott took the party further right and weaponised ideological conflict. Malcolm Turnbull, though personally progressive, failed to bring the party with him. Scott Morrison replaced substance with slogans and ran a government mired in secrecy, incompetence, and scandal. And then came Dutton—a figure more feared than respected, and ultimately unable to bring the party out of its culture war death spiral.

Now the blame game had begun. Former staffers and insiders pointed to the lack of economic credibility, the absence of serious policy costings, and an election campaign that felt reactive and unfocused. There was plenty of blame to go around—and while Dutton was the obvious target, he should not have been the only one. The rot had been systemic, stretching back over a decade or more, across multiple leaders and factions.

The Liberal Party's fall was not inevitable—but it was well deserved. Unless it faced up to the full scale of its collapse, it would never recover as a major political force. And perhaps the hardest part of all: the Liberal Party had to learn how to *listen*. Listen to the electorate, not just the loudest voices in the media, and not just regurgitate the noise from these voices as culture war garbage. Listen to communities. Listen to critics. Listen to those who had left the party—and those who might be willing to return, if there were something worth returning to.

THE POWER OF THE MANDATE

The Labor government emerged from the 2025 federal election with an overwhelming level of political capital—perhaps more than any progressive government in the post-war period. For the Prime Minister, Anthony Albanese, this was not just a personal triumph but a vindication of the cautious and steady first-term strategy that built credibility, trust, and stability within a volatile political environment. While much had been made of his declining personal approval in the eighteen months leading up to the election, the election result suggested that electoral success did not necessarily depend on personal popularity—the opinion polls, as they so often did, proved to be a blunt and unreliable instrument. Albanese might not have inspired the admiration that was once reserved for leaders such as Bob Hawke or Kevin Rudd, but he secured something far more important: a strong and workable majority built on respect, steadiness, and competence.

In hindsight, his measured approach to governing with a slim three-seat majority during the first term seemed not only reasonable but strategically sound. Labor's first-term caution was less about timidity and more about establishing the groundwork for long-term reform—reassuring a skeptical electorate that it could trust a federal Labor government again after a decade of Coalition incompetence and Labor's own brand of political mayhem that preceded that. But now, with that trust banked and a commanding mandate in hand, there was no purpose in preserving political capital just for its own sake. Power, once it was given by the electorate, needed to be exercised with *purpose*. Otherwise, what was the point of having it?

This moment presented both an opportunity and a risk. Albanese's leadership style—deliberate, consultative and unflashy—didn't deliver sky-high approval ratings, but it might have proved to be more durable in the long run. Unlike Rudd, whose approval ratings hit stratospheric heights before collapsing under the weight of internal ambition and instability, Albanese was unlikely to inspire a cult of personality, nor did he appear to seek one. He understood the structural safeguards that were put in place after having been a front seat witness during the Rudd–Gillard–Rudd era—the so-called "Rudd rules" that required two-thirds of Caucus support to dislodge a sitting Prime Minister—that made leadership spills difficult and politically costly. In such a context, the allure of charismatic popularity was not only unnecessary, it might have ended up being totally counterproductive.

Given the size of this election result, some Labor Party strategists might have already been contemplating the 2028 election. However, some of that planning may have been put on hold when factional machinations played out in a very public and brutal way immediately after the election, where Deputy Prime Minister Richard Marles used his undeserved influence to force Attorney-General Mark Dreyfus and Minister for Industry and Science Ed Husic out of the Cabinet. While Dreyfus might have been considering retirement after eighteen years in politics anyway, Husic had proven to be a competent minister and had built a strong link between the government and Islamic communities in Western Sydney—a relationship that was damaged by the government's one-sided support of Israel's actions in Palestine. It was an unnecessary and public act, coming just days after an election victory that generated significant electoral goodwill, but clearly not much factional goodwill for these two Cabinet members.

History suggested that governments typically performed best at their first term and started to accumulate problems at their second. This factional mismanagement would be forgotten about soon enough but the challenge now was for the government to plan not just for consolidation but for strategic building: to expect attrition in some marginal seats while identifying new opportunities to compensate for inevitable losses that were likely to happen at the next election. A large mandate and a one-sided electoral victory could invite complacency—but it could also enable boldness, reform, and renewal.

THE POLITICS OF OPPORTUNITY AND RISK

The Labor government now found itself in a historically favourable political position—arguably the strongest position the federal Labor Party had ever had. With a commanding lower house seat tally estimated to be 94—well above the 76-seat threshold required to govern—and a fractured, demoralised opposition in disarray, the scale of Labor's authority couldn't be overstated. Not only was the Coalition facing a devastating loss of influence and parliamentary talent, but the additional buffer created by the crossbench—albeit somewhat weakened following losses by community independents and the Australian Greens—left the Albanese government with an extraordinary advantage. The gap between Labor and the Coalition now sat at nearly fifty seats, a wide electoral gap that gave the government immense freedom to legislate and govern with confidence.

The Senate was also more manageable than in recent terms: although Labor did not have outright control of the upper house, it only required the support of the Australian Greens to pass legislation—while the relationship with the Greens was often strained and tenuous, this was far more preferable than having to negotiate with a rag-tag of unaligned and unpredictable Senators from other parties. Relatively speaking, this was a dream scenario for a Labor government, and one that opened the door to meaningful reform. Yet within this abundance lay danger: political capital, like any other form of capital, was only valuable when used *wisely*. The temptation to play it safe, to coast on the momentum of victory, should have been set aside: caution and consolidation had already served their purpose; that was what got Albanese to this point in his political career. For this next parliamentary term, a boldness of clarity, discipline and strategic intelligence, should define the actions of the government.

While Labor faced an opportunity to reshape Australia in its own image, the spectre of overreach loomed. The example of John Howard after his 2004 landslide hovered over this parliament like Banquo's ghost: a thumping majority, control of the Senate, and a government emboldened to push WorkChoices and a raft of neoliberal policies that ultimately alienated voters and led to a crushing defeat in 2007. That was a textbook example of how *not* to use political capital. But the reforms Labor was likely to pursue—targeted taxation reform, changes to negative gearing and capital gains tax, revitalising public housing, increasing mining royalties, and boosting higher education, were not ideological overreaches: they were rooted in long-standing Labor values and would have broad public support if framed effectively and supported with a coherent political narrative.

For sure, these measures did not feature in the 2025 campaign—but neither did WorkChoices in 2004. The difference was intent and transparency. If Labor moved with clarity, delicate political positioning, and public explanation, these policies could build long-term support and deliver tangible results. The electorate, more than ever, wanted government to act *in the national interest*, not just to maintain a façade of fiscal caution or political indifference. The task was not to shock the electorate, but to prepare them for how Labor's values and programs could translate into outcomes that improved lives.

Beyond domestic policy, foreign affairs remained a mixed bag. Australia's relationships with Indonesia and the South Pacific were strong; relations with China had been stabilised. But the AUKUS pact negotiated by Scott Morrison was still a multi-billion-dollar question—widely criticised for its outrageous cost and lack of clear strategic goals, its cancellation or overhaul might have been controversial but ultimately defensible, particularly if those funds were redirected into public health or education. Likewise, the Labor government needed to confront the deep inconsistency in its Middle East policy. Vague equivocations over Israel–Palestine risked undermining the values Labor claimed to uphold, particularly when Israel's human rights violations and war crimes became impossible to ignore. At the very least, the government had to develop a consistent and ethical approach to international diplomacy, one that was not shaped solely by strategic alliances or domestic political caution.

Ultimately, what Labor needed most was coherence: a policy vision grounded in *equity* and *fairness*—traditional Labor values—that could be applied across housing, taxation, foreign affairs, climate, and social services. There was no serious threat from the opposition for the foreseeable future, and no need to govern in fear of political retribution from either the Coalition or a feckless mainstream media. But this situation wouldn't last forever. The time was very favourable to use political capital for structural reform—not *reckless* adventurism, but *principled* ambition.

Housing stood out as the single most transformative issue that could have become a great legacy for this Labor government. It could begin reversing decades of neglect by investing directly in public housing—not as a market supplement, but as a fundamental solution to widespread inequality. Public housing worked: study after study showed it alleviated homelessness, reduced pressure on the rental market, and restored dignity to those priced out of the private market. If Labor wanted to be remembered as more than a cautious keeper of the political centre, it had to be willing to offend some of the vested interests in real estate, construction industries and finance. Votes might be lost in parts of the upper middle class in future elections, but the reward—material, political, and moral—would far outweigh the cost.

With a decisive mandate, a demoralised and disorganised opposition, and a Parliament overwhelmingly favourable to progressive reform, the Labor government reached political heights rarely seen in Australian political history. This was not the time to govern timidly or limit ambition to a narrow list of pre-election commitments. Australia couldn't wait. Circumstances would shift. The economy, society, and global order would all evolve—often in unpredictable ways—and the Albanese government had to be ready to respond not just with managerial competence, but with a compelling reform agenda that shaped the future. Albanese had the chance to enter the pantheon of great Labor leaders—not just as the leader who achieved a massive election victory, but the one who made that victory matter.

EPILOGUE

The 2025 election will, in retrospect, be seen as even more important than the 2022 contest. It wasn't just the records it set—the largest Labor Party majority in decades, the worst ever result for the Liberal Party, the catastrophic loss of three Australian Greens lower house seats despite a stable vote, and the loss of independent senators, while maintaining a stable number of independents in the House of Representatives. Its true significance lies in the primary vote: just 35 per cent for Labor and 32 per cent for the Coalition. This is where the importance of 2025 becomes clear.

The major parties in Australia have experienced a long and steady decline. Since the 1980s, party membership has been in terminal decline, and the political tribalism that once defined Australian politics—since at least Federation in 1901—has significantly weakened. Today, a much larger share of the electorate is made up of undecided voters: people who vote based on issues or outcomes rather than longstanding party loyalty. Even minor parties like the Greens are not immune—what appears to be a strong base may not be as stable as it seems.

EPILOGUE

DECLINING PARTY MEMBERSHIP

In the 1950s, the Liberal Party of Australia boasted around 197,000 members. By 2020, that number had dropped to about 40,000. Labor has experienced a similar trend, now sitting at around 60,000 members. In a voting population of over 18 million, this is almost statistically insignificant. The National Party claims roughly 9,000 members and is virtually non-existent outside Queensland, New South Wales, and northern Victoria. It's also notable that most independents in the House won their seats from sitting Liberal members and were able to retain them.

This membership decline stems from a number of factors. One of the most significant is neoliberalism, particularly the Thatcherite idea that "there's no such thing as society," which has eroded community participation. Younger generations now gather more online than locally. While most political parties maintain youth wings (for those under twenty-five or thirty), these groups are facing the same decline as their parent branches. The trend appears terminal.

Our society—particularly in capitalist, democratic Western nations—has fractured into isolated nuclear families, with a less perceived need to congregate around shared interests. Contributing factors include increased work hours and time pressures that make evening or weekend participation in party events difficult. Young families are less likely to "get involved," meaning children aren't exposed to community or political engagement through their parents.

THE EXISTENTIAL CRISIS OF THE MAJOR PARTIES

The Australian Labor Party was founded in the 1890s following a series of failed strikes, created to give the working class a voice in Parliament. Although it has splintered over ideological issues several times, its core mission was always to represent the industrial working class.

The Liberal Party, meanwhile, emerged as a coalition of Free Traders and Protectionists—a formation designed primarily to keep the "socialist" Labor Party out of office. It has undergone several reconfigurations, most notably in 1944 when the old United Australia Party was transformed into the Liberal Party of Australia. It stemmed from an Edwardian philosophy of progressivism.

By 1977, both parties had adopted versions of neoliberalism. Bill Hayden became Labor leader, while John Howard was appointed Federal Treasurer. Regardless of interpretation, both major parties are now based on outdated concepts of how society and economics should function. Their efforts to modernise have mostly resulted in superficial reforms and both are out of step with public sentiment—on climate change, foreign policy, and social issues.

The AUKUS agreement should have been abandoned already, yet both major parties continue to support it. No wonder the 'Teal' independents—community-backed candidates financially supported by Simon Holmes à Court—found success, especially in historically safe Liberal seats like Wentworth and Kooyong. Their primary concerns—climate change and women's rights—resonated with voters, especially given the Liberal Party's poor record on gender issues. Consider the treatment of Brittany

Higgins, Julia Banks, and others who never made headlines. Under Menzies, women arguably had better treatment—he appointed the first female federal minister and ensured women's contributions to the party were acknowledged.

Labor fares better on gender equality, with women currently making up 52 per cent of the Cabinet and 57 per cent of Caucus, a better reflection of modern Australian society. But not all sexist behaviour targeting women—like Julia Gillard—came from the Opposition. Misogyny is not eradicated, but a modern party must reflect progressive values or take a lead in shaping them. The election of Sussan Ley to the Liberal leadership was a positive step, though her long-term viability remains in question. She has already been undermined by those within her own party, dog-whistling that she won't last long.

ENVIRONMENTAL AND ECONOMIC FAILURES

Both major parties have failed on the environment. Labor approved many new coal mines, even as the rest of the world moves away from fossil fuels. The Liberals, meanwhile, proposed nuclear power—a solution that would take at least twenty years (likely more) to implement, cost significantly more than renewables, and face major waste and safety concerns. By the time any nuclear generators came online, they would likely be obsolete. Many analysts viewed this as a cynical ploy to prolong coal's relevance.

Labor must also rethink its approach to industrial relations. While collective bargaining is inherently fairer, union membership is at historic lows, and the twentieth-century union model no longer fits today's job market. Most employment is now temporary, casual, or precarious. This has created issues around affordability, security, and stability. The gig economy is failing—ideally, it should be limited to casual weekend or evening work for students and young workers.

While the 2025 election was a remarkable victory for the Australian Labor Party, the key challenge now is to avoid complacency and a fear of bold action. Labor must use its political capital to make meaningful improvements for all Australians. Ironically, it may have won power at a time demanding deep and necessary transformation. We are possibly witnessing the death of the Liberal Party—and perhaps the birth of an entirely new political system. But we should beware the death throes of those who benefited from the old ways; their grip on power can be hard to break. The 2025 election may have shown us a glimpse of Australia's political future. The red wave may have washed away more than anyone expected.

INDEX OF PEOPLE

A

Tony Abbott 26, 28, 78, 118, 175, 198, 205, 227, 236
David Adler 108
Anthony Albanese 6, 7, 10, 11, 12, 13, 15, 16, 17, 18, 22, 23, 24, 25, 26, 27, 34, 41, 43, 47, 48, 51, 52, 53, 56, 57, 65, 68, 79, 81, 86, 89, 90, 93, 94, 97, 98, 101, 103, 111, 112, 116, 124, 128, 130, 131, 133, 134, 135, 136, 137, 138, 144, 145, 147, 148, 152, 159, 160, 161, 162, 164, 165, 168, 169, 171, 177, 179, 181, 191, 192, 195, 196, 197, 199, 200, 215, 216, 217, 218, 221, 222, 223, 224, 237, 238, 240, 243, 252
Tim Anderson 71, 72
Bridget Archer 223

B

Adam Bandt 166, 167, 168
Julia Banks 247
Natalie Barr 111
Ziad Basyouny 131
Joe Biden 47, 51
Ofir Birenbaum 66, 67
Tony Blair 48
Alan Bond 155
Chris Bowen 135
George W. Bush 55, 90

C

Jim Chalmers 93, 112, 120, 121, 128, 129, 221
Bill Clinton 10, 48
Eldbridge Colby 88
James Cook 29
Roger Cook 90
Peta Credlin 230
John Curtin 222

D

Mark Dreyfus 239
Peter Dutton 7, 11, 12, 14, 15, 16, 17, 18, 19, 20, 21, 22, 23, 24, 25, 26, 27, 28, 30, 31, 34, 45, 46, 47, 48, 51, 54, 63, 64, 75, 77, 78, 79, 81, 82, 83, 86, 97, 98, 99, 100, 102, 103, 110, 111, 112, 113, 114, 115, 116, 117, 118, 129, 130, 133, 134, 135, 137, 138, 139, 140, 141, 142, 143, 144, 145, 146, 147, 148, 149, 150, 152, 156, 157, 159, 160, 161, 162, 170, 171, 172, 174, 175, 176, 177, 179, 180, 181, 191, 192, 193, 194, 195, 196, 197, 199, 205, 215, 216, 217, 218, 219, 220, 221, 222, 224, 225, 226, 227, 229, 230, 232, 233, 235, 236

E

H.V. Evatt 174, 176

F

Ali France 137, 222
Josh Frydenberg 137

G

Julia Gillard 78, 81, 156, 176, 198, 238, 247

H

Andrew Hastie 193, 195
Bob Hawke 16, 48, 237
Bill Hayden 246
Justin Hemmes 111
John Hewson 82, 145, 174, 176
Brittany Higgins 246
Adolf Hitler 40
Simon Holmes à Court 246
John Howard 8, 19, 20, 49, 100, 154, 174, 182, 185, 203, 227, 231, 236, 240, 246
Ed Husic 239

J

Boris Johnson 46

K

Patricia Karvelas 136
Bob Katter 78
Paul Keating 16, 42, 48, 77, 81, 132
Mahmoud Khalil 106
King George III 32

L

Ally Langdon 196
David Lange 57

Mark Latham 174
Antoinette Lattouf 71
Julian Leeser 108
Sussan Ley 30, 114, 230, 233, 234, 235, 247
Simon Love 136
Joe Lyons 222

M
Richard Marles 56, 238
James McGrath 221
Teena McQueen 232
Robert Menzies 121, 203, 222, 227, 228, 247
Chris Minns 69, 103, 104
Scott Morrison 11, 20, 46, 54, 57, 88, 93, 94, 112, 118, 123, 136, 172, 173, 175, 198, 199, 205, 215, 216, 219, 220, 236, 241, 252
Rupert Murdoch 30, 67, 175, 230
Paul Murray 230
Elon Musk 30, 39, 45
Benito Mussolini 40

N
Benjamin Netanyahu 166

O
Rob Oakeshott 78
Ted O'Brien 234
Clare O'Neil 181

P
Kerry Packer 155
Rita Panahi 232
James Paterson 103
Vladimir Petrov 174
Governor Arthur Phillip 32
Tanya Plibersek 179
Pope Francis 191, 199
Jacinta Price 45, 233, 235

R
Gina Rinehart 46, 130, 154, 196
Andrew Robb 153
Jay Rosen 76
Kevin Rudd 57, 81, 156, 198, 237, 238
Monique Ryan 136, 138

S
Khaled Sabsabi 71

SaVĀge K'lub 72
Bill Shorten 82, 136, 171, 177, 198, 215
Rod Sims 135
Ellie Smith 137
Keir Starmer 47, 51, 88
Alexa Stuart 161

T
Angus Taylor 96, 124, 129, 156, 233, 235
Margaret Thatcher 48, 49, 184
Justin Trudeau 84
Donald Trump 7, 23, 36, 37, 38, 39, 40, 41, 43, 44, 45, 46, 48, 51, 52, 53, 54, 55, 57, 88, 89, 90, 98, 99, 100, 101, 115, 116, 117, 131, 145, 224, 232
Melania Trump 39
Malcolm Turnbull 140, 175, 177, 205, 236

V
J.D. Vance 90

W
Tim Wilson 233, 234, 235
Tony Windsor 78
Keith Wolahan 223
Penny Wong 108, 164, 167

Z
Volodymyr Zelenskyy 88

ALSO BY
EDDY JOKOVICH + DAVID LEWIS

THE AGE OF DISAPPOINTMENT: THE REVIEW OF THE YEAR IN AUSTRALIAN POLITICS

FIXING AUSTRALIAN POLITICS
HOW TO CHANGE THE SYSTEM OF GOVERNMENT

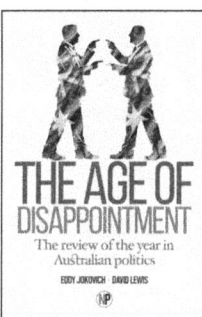

From the timidity of the Labor Party and the crisis facing the Liberals, to the rise of independents and challenges within the Greens, *The Age of Disappointment* explores the shifting sands of Australian politics—the missed opportunities of the Albanese government, the cynicism of Dutton's opposition, and the public's growing disconnection from traditional power structures. Beyond Australia, the book examines the global zeitgeist reshaping Western democracies, the ramifications of Trump's re-election in the U.S. and the controversial support for Israel government, set against the backdrop of an increasingly disillusioned electorate.

Available in paperback and ebook.

The Age of Disappointment: The review of the year in Australian politics
ISBN (paperback): 978-1-7635701-2-2
ISBN (Amazon): 979-8-3025811-6-7
404 pages

Australia's political landscape stands on the precipice of transformation. The need for reform is palpable, driven by evolving societal values, demands for greater transparency, and a push towards inclusivity. *Fixing Australian Politics: How to change the system of government* outlines a multifaceted strategy to reshape Australian politics across various fronts—electoral systems, campaign finance, governance, media, the Constitution, and diversity in representation. These reforms are critical for the rejuvenation of the nation's political framework and the restoration of public faith in the democratic process.

Available in paperback and ebook.

Fixing Australian Politics: How to change the system of government
ISBN (paperback): 978-1-7635701-0-8
ISBN (Amazon): 979-8-3249179-2-0
208 pages

RISING PHOENIX, FALLING SHADOWS

THE YEAR IN AUSTRALIAN POLITICS

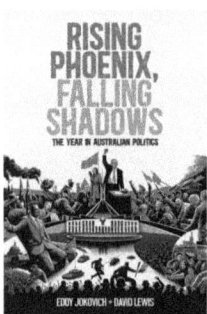

This exploration of Australia's political landscape in 2023 uncovers a year that began with high hopes, yet was marred by a series of unmet expectations and enduring challenges: the Voice to Parliament referendum and its subsequent defeat, the persistent housing crisis, cost of living and environmental concerns, AUKUS and Palestine—guiding the reader through the intricate web of political and social dynamics that define contemporary Australia. *Rising Phoenix, Falling Shadows* is a compelling read for anyone interested in understanding the multifaceted nature of governance and public policy in Australia.

Available in paperback and ebook.

Rising Phoenix, Falling Shadows: The year in Australian politics
ISBN (paperback): 978-0-6456392-9-2
ISBN (Amazon): 979-8-8720426-0-0
446 pages

DIARY OF AN ELECTION VICTORY

LABOR'S RISE TO POWER

In early 2020 at the onset of the coronavirus pandemic, Morrison held record high electoral ratings and Albanese was told to not worry about the next election: it was already out of reach and best to focus on the 2025 election and beyond. In 2022, Labor saw an opportunity: Morrison had made promises he ultimately couldn't deliver and it unravelled quickly. *Diary of An Election Victory* explores the key political moments of the 2022 election year, Morrison's demise, and Albanese's ascendancy and victory against the odds. It's a must-read analysis of one of the most dynamic and unusual election results ever in Australia's political history.

Available in paperback and ebook.

Diary of an Election Victory:
ISBN (paperback): 978-0-6456392-1-6
ISBN (hardback): 978-0-6456392-2-3
ISBN (Amazon): 979-8-3681569-7-2
304 pages

POLITICS, PROTEST, PANDEMIC

THE YEAR THAT CHANGED AUSTRALIA

2020 was one of the most dramatic years in human history, shaped by the coronavirus pandemic that influenced society in so many different ways, combining health, politics, economics, business and education into the one sphere—and that proved to be difficult for many governments around the world to manage. *Politics, Protest, Pandemic: The year that changed Australia* is the story of the year in Australian federal politics, told through a collection of extended political essays from the New Politics Australia podcast series. This is a must-read analysis of one of the most dynamic years ever in Australian political history.

Available in paperback and ebook.

Politics, Protest, Pandemic: The year that changed Australia
ISBN: 978-0-6481644-8-7
ISBN (Amazon): 979-8-7372030-8-5
414 pages

DIVIDED OPINIONS

THE NEW POLITICS ANALYSIS OF THE 2019 YEAR IN AUSTRALIAN POLITICS

As the mainstream media struggles to retain audiences and survive under new business models and shrinking revenue streams, independents are filling in the gaps left behind by the older mastheads. New Politics is one of the more important voices appearing in this new landscape, and *Divided Opinions* presents some of the best work from the monthly podcast, and a selection of articles published during 2019. Guaranteed to make you think; aggravate, or inform and enlighten—and maybe all at once—this is a must-read analysis of one of the most dynamic years ever in Australian politics.

Available in paperback and ebook.

Divided Opinions: The New Politics analysis of the 2019 year in Australian politics
ISBN: 978-0-6481644-5-6
ISBN (Amazon): 978-1-6611355-7-7
338 pages

www.ingramcontent.com/pod-product-compliance
Lightning Source LLC
Chambersburg PA
CBHW031146020426
42333CB00013B/535